TWISTED

TWISTED

TALES FROM THE WACKY SIDE OF LIFE

BOB FENSTER

**Andrews McMeel
Publishing, LLC**

Kansas City

06 07 08 09 10 RR2 10 9 8 7 6 5 4 3 2 1

ISBN-13: 978-0-7407-6050-1
ISBN-10: 0-7407-6050-5

Library of Congress Control Number: 2006922719

www.andrewsmcmeel.com

Book design by Holly Camerlinck

ATTENTION: SCHOOLS AND BUSINESSES
Andrews McMeel books are available at quantity discounts with bulk purchase for educational, business, or sales promotional use. For information, please write to: Special Sales Department, Andrews McMeel Publishing, LLC, 4520 Main Street, Kansas City, Missouri 64111.

This book is dedicated to Anne Bothwell,
who was a straight-A student until she ran into me.

CONTENTS

TWELVE

Into the Harem and Other Twisted Surprises

THIRTEEN

Imaginary Pebbles and Pet Lobsters:
The Weird Habits of Highly Strange People

FOURTEEN

Redesigning the Sky: Twisted Egos of the Stars

FIFTEEN

On to Paradise: Hidden Meanings and Odd Origins

SIXTEEN

Inside Hollyweird: Behind the Scenes in La-La Land

SEVENTEEN

Driving in Turkmenistan: The Odds Against Us

EIGHTEEN

Aimless Wandering and Other Obvious Things
That Are Not What They Appear to Be

INTRODUCTION

"Never make people laugh," Congressman Thomas Corwin advised. "If you would succeed in life, you must be solemn, solemn as an ass. All the great monuments are built over solemn asses."

Congressman Corwin was being funny when he advised against being funny. He knew that laughter is the opposite of making sense.

If you listen to the volunteer hall monitors of the world, everything makes perfect sense. But that's not where the interesting thinking goes on. For those moments in life that make you laugh, you need the eccentrics, the original thinkers, the congressmen, and other nutjobs. Fortunately, the human race is the world's leading producer of the twisted and the wacky.

This book is a collection of the funny things people do when they stray from the line and tap into the 90 percent of the mind that we don't usually use.

Going off-center gets us originals like these:

John Norbury and John Parsons, two Irish lawyers of the 1700s, were riding in their carriage past a scaffold upon which a criminal had been hung.

"If we all had our deserts," Norbury challenged his companion, "where would you be?"

Parsons glanced at his friend and said, "Riding alone in my carriage."

French scientists established the Guzman Prize in 1900, putting up 100,000 francs for the first person who could establish communications with extraterrestrials.

The scientists who served as contest judges ruled that contacting Martians would not qualify for the prize, because that was too easy.

No report on how much money the Martians offered their scientists for discovering intelligent life on Earth.

Life isn't always funny. We learn this from watching TV sitcoms. The serious parts of life are easy. You can't miss them, and they probably won't miss you. Real-life comedy? A little harder to find. But life is funny when you least expect it—and when you probably need it the most.

Perhaps you're rich, beautiful, and adored. But probably not. Perhaps you have something people usually aren't adored for: a twisted mind. You will never get elected president of the In-Crowd. But you are ready to join the Pantheon of the Eccentrics. Look at the company you'll keep:

Originals like the seventeenth-century French scholar Baron de Montesquieu, who pointed out, "If triangles made a god, they would give him three sides."

Or painter Salvador Dali, who once gave a speech all politicians should memorize. He stepped up to the dais and said, "I will be so brief I have already finished." And he was.

Or Korean distance runner Kitei Song, who trained for the 1936 Olympics by running in baggy pants, his pockets filled with sand, and rocks tied to his back.

Just as stupidity is good for the economy, wackiness is a growth industry. Comedians would be unemployed if they didn't have fools and idiots to make fun of. Newspapers would be blanks with ads.

But we'll be OK as long as we listen to the odd ones, like comic Monica Piper who explained why juries scare her: "I don't want to put my fate in the hands of twelve people who weren't smart enough to get out of jury duty."

Life doesn't have a laugh quota. Grab as many as you can. If you miss a few, remember what my uncle Jackamon Jakowski told me when I went into this funny business. "Bob," he said, "they're going to call you crazy. And they're probably right."

When you start from that position, it's hard to go wrong.

My search for the comedy of real life began with a stupid idea: I wondered if the dueling forces of progress and absurdity were stretching our minds in two directions at the same time — so that the stupidity of the human race increased at the same rate as our intelligence?

Since my books draw their laughs from real life, people often ask if the world is going to run out of material for me. And I say, "Not if you pitch in and do something funny today."

So let's move it, people! Some serious stuff has been spotted in your town. Let's get out there and twist it.

PART I

ONE

THE DEAR JOHN INFOMERCIAL: STRANGE STRATEGIES FOR DEALING WITH THE WEIRD CHALLENGES OF LIFE

"Never sleep with anyone whose troubles are worse than your own," mystery writer Ross Macdonald suggested. Good advice, but try to follow it.

Sometimes a reasonable approach actually works. Just as often, brains fail. Advisers stink. Planning, courage, luck—strike one, two, three. At times like these, doing the strangest thing you can think of may be all that saves you.

"Run always after a dog, he'll never bite you," recommended François Rabelais, the French writer of the bizarre. "Drink always before a thirst, and it will never overtake you."

"Buy land," writer Mark Twain advised investors. "They've stopped making it."

> IF YOU DON'T HAVE THE MONEY TO BUY LAND,
> TRY THIS STRATEGY FROM COMIC
> STEVEN WRIGHT: "BORROW MONEY FROM
> PESSIMISTS. THEY DON'T EXPECT IT BACK."

Model Liz Fuller asked her boyfriend, hypnotist Paul McKenna, to watch her appearance on the TV show, *Auction World,* in 2004. During an auction of engagement rings, Fuller looked into the camera and told McKenna she was leaving him.

As she closed the bidding on a ring, she called: "Going, going, gone. Just like you, Paul."

Thus, the Dear John letter has been replaced not only by the Dear John e-mail, but also by the Dear John infomercial.

Julia, daughter of the Roman Emperor Augustus Caesar, was notorious for her love affairs. A friend expressed surprise that all five of Julia's children looked like her husband, Marcus Agrippa.

Julia had a simple explanation: "Passengers are never allowed on board until the hold is full."

There are people who fight their duels with great courage and skill. Others don't need skills. They have cunning.

1)   Before he became an American commander in the Revolutionary War, Israel Putnam fought alongside the British in the French and Indian War. An arrogant major in the British regulars challenged Putnam to a duel.

Because he had choice of weapons and knew the other man was a better shot, Putnam dared his foe to engage in a version of eighteenth-century chicken. The two men would sit opposite each other on powder kegs, and then light the fuses. Whoever jumped off and ran first would lose the test of courage.

When the major saw the witnesses backing away and Putnam settling back on his keg to light a pipe, he knew he was beaten. He ran off before the kegs exploded.

That's when Putnam opened the kegs to reveal they contained not gunpowder but onions.

2) German scientist Rudolf Virchano had the temerity to criticize hot-tempered Chancellor Otto von Bismarck, who challenged him to a duel.

Knowing of Bismarck's prowess with pistol and sword, the scientist chose as their weapons — sausages. One, he explained was infected with deadly germs; the other, perfectly edible.

"Let His Excellency do me the honor to choose whichever he wishes and eat it," Virchano offered. "I will eat the other."

Bismarck, realizing that discretion was the better part of dinner, declined the duel.

3) In 1808 two Parisians fought a duel with muskets in hot-air balloons. One man shot the other's balloon, and his rival died in the plunge.

4) When eighteenth-century American lawyer Hugh Brackenridge was challenged to a duel, he came up with this unique response: "If you want to try your pistols, take some object, a tree or a barn door, about my dimensions. If you hit that, send me word; and I shall acknowledge that if I had been in the same place, you might also have hit me."

5) As a young man, French Prime Minister Georges Clemenceau fought several duels. As he went off to face a challenge, a friend was surprised when Clemenceau bought a one-way ticket at the train station. The friend asked Clemenceau if he felt that pessimistic about his chances.

"Not at all," Clemenceau responded happily. "I always use my opponent's return ticket for the trip back."

In Hans Christian Andersen's fairy tales, people facing unusual problems find magical solutions. As a young man, Andersen had his own problems. He was so thin and weak that friends worried about his health.

Andersen wished to appear manly, but he didn't have three magic wishes. Instead, he came up with an unusual solution: before going out in public, he would stuff newspapers into his shirt.

Self-doubt afflicted many writers, from Ernest Hemingway to Norman Mailer, none of whom thought of the newspaper-in-the-shirt ploy. Instead, they took to drinking bouts or boxing bouts—or one after the other—to demonstrate that they were men's men even if they did type for a living.

Billionaire H. L. Hunt believed the American system of one person-one vote was inherently unfair. He proposed a new system where the more money you had, the more votes you could cast.

Hunt's electoral system was not adopted, because no one else was rich enough to vote for it. But something similar remains in effect: the more money candidates can invest in their election campaigns, the more likely they are to win office.

Saint Bernard of Clairvaux grew tired of swatting at flies, and who hasn't? Then he had a brainstorm and tried a new approach: he excommunicated all the flies flitting about his monastery. When that strategy didn't eliminate the enemy, he went back to his fly swatter.

A sportswriter asked baseball manager Alvin Dark to compare the teams he had led over his years in the game.

"With the A's we depended upon pitching and speed to win," Dark said. "With the Giants we had pitching and power. With the Indians we depended upon an act of God."

Financier Jay Gould advised the rector of his church to invest his life's savings in a particular stock. After putting all his money into the stock, the rector was shocked to see it take a steep dive. His life savings were wiped out.

As the man tried to figure out what to do, Gould handed him a check to cover all the money he'd lost. Thanking the millionaire, the rector admitted that he had told several members of his congregation about Gould's tip, and they had lost all their money too.

"I know," Gould said. "They were the ones I was after."

The avant-garde Futurist movement of the early 1900s produced concerts throughout Europe that infuriated music lovers with a mix of music and noise.

After several hostile receptions, Futurist composer Luigi Russolo had his orchestra trained by professional boxers prior to a concert in Paris.

During the performance, angry audience members attacked the musicians. While half the orchestra played on, the other half counterattacked. The result? A TKO for the Futurists, with eleven audience members sent to the hospital.

IN SIXTEENTH-CENTURY EUROPE, FLEA COATS BECAME A FASHIONABLE, YET PRACTICAL ACCESSORY. MADE FROM HEAVY FUR, THE FLEA COAT WAS WORN TO DRAW THE FLEAS INTO THE COAT AND OFF YOUR SKIN.

In ancient Rome, court officials used water clocks to time the speeches given by lawyers for either side of a dispute. The court was attempting to keep the speeches equal in length if not oratory prowess.

But leave it to lawyers to come up with a clever way to gain an advantage from equality. A smart Roman lawyer would bribe the timekeeper to put mud in the water during his turn, to slow down the clock and give him more time to sway the judges.

> WHEN AVIATION ENTHUSIAST HOWARD HUGHES SET OUT TO BREAK THE SPEED RECORD FOR CIRCLING THE GLOBE IN 1938, HE HAD HIS PLANE FILLED WITH PING-PONG BALLS. WHY? SO IT WOULD FLOAT IF FORCED TO MAKE AN EMERGENCY LANDING IN THE OCEAN.

In the 1950s proper middle-class women did not dye their hair. Clairol wanted to convince them that changing hair color was not something only "bad girls" did, a notion made popular by Hollywood and "bad girls."

To win over suburban women and open a vast new market for hair dyes, Clairol came up with an ad campaign considered suggestive at the time: "Does she . . . or doesn't she?" In the ads only her hairdresser knew for sure.

Life, the most popular magazine in the United States, refused to run the ad, claiming the sexual innuendo was too licentious.

Clairol execs got *Life*'s management (mostly men) to ask their women staffers (mostly secretaries) if they found anything naughty in the ads. Not wanting to embarrass themselves, the *Life* women found the ad innocent of all erotic innuendo.

Life magazine ran the ad. Millions of American women took to dyeing their hair, and Clairol made a fortune. To maintain the claim of innocence in their risqué ads, Clairol always included a photo of a child looking proud that her mother had finally dyed her hair. Women, the ad inferred, were dyeing their hair not to attract men but to keep the kids happy.

Writer Florence King revealed a surprising strategy for men who didn't fit into traditional roles. "For men who want to flee Family Man America and never come back," she said, "there is a guaranteed solution. Homosexuality is the new French Foreign Legion."

Those who seek adventure and new thrills: Before you head off to exotic realms, take a tip from the quiet strategy of writer Marcel Proust: "The voyage of discovery is not in seeking new landscapes, but in having new eyes."

Playwright Arthur Miller married the movie bombshell Marilyn Monroe, thus becoming the only playwright ever envied by most of the guys in America.

Miller developed a marital strategy that all guys who plan to marry the sexiest woman in America might want to follow: "All my energy and attention were devoted to trying to help her solve her problems," he said. "Unfortunately, I didn't have much success."

The problem with following the obvious solution is that you may end up in a crowd with all the others who went for the obvious. At those times, the counterintuitive is your best bet.

For example, when you walk into a large public restroom, the kind you find at airports, which stall should you choose?

The one closest to the door. It's the one most people won't take, so it's the cleanest.

When George Eastman invented the world's easiest and most popular camera, he wanted to give it a name that started and ended with the letter K. Why K? Because "it seems a strong, incisive letter," Eastman claimed.

With first and last letters in place, Eastman simply filled in the spaces between with various combinations of letters until he arrived at one that worked: Kodak.

The Swiss artist Paul Klee signed his paintings with a clover instead of his name. In German *klee* means, you guessed it, "clover."

Athletes choose their uniform numbers for such ordinary reasons as it was worn by a childhood favorite. But not all of them. Some athletes choose oddly:

1) Miami Dolphins quarterback Dan Marino wore No. 13—not because he was defying superstition, but because no one else would.

   When Dan played Little League baseball, his dad coached the team and let the other players choose their uniforms ahead of his son. When it finally got to Dan's turn, there was only one shirt left: No. 13.

2) Cleveland Indians outfielder Paul Dade wore No. oo to remind himself that during the baseball draft only two teams showed interest in him, and neither of them was very interested. "Nobody really wanted me," Dade recalled. "I figured nothing for nothing equals two zeroes."

3) Jan Stenerud, who kicked field goals for the NFL's Kansas City Chiefs, chose No. 3 for two reasons (would have been more appropriate if he had three reasons).

   First, he wanted to score three points each time he kicked a field goal. Second, Stenerud followed a superstition before each kick: tapping his foot on the ground three times.

4) New York Giants pitcher Bill Voiselle wore No. 96. Baseball

numbers rarely go that high. But Voiselle came from an unusual town in South Carolina named Ninety Six.

When a baseball player joins another team, his favorite uniform number may already be taken. Then he may try to buy the number from the current holder.

When pitcher Mitch Williams joined the Philadelphia Phillies in 1991, slugger John Kruk already wore his favorite: No. 28. Negotiations commenced. Kruk finally sold the number to Williams for two cases of beer.

"I knew it would be beer or Ding Dongs," Williams said of the portly Kruk. "I just didn't know which."

Movie star George Clooney has a funny way of keeping his life in balance: "It's important to remember that you're never as good as they say you are when they say you're good and never as bad as they say you are when they say you're bad. Eventually, I'll be doing infomercials, so it won't matter anyhow."

Long before he became president, Franklin Roosevelt worked as a trial lawyer. During one of his first civil cases, he realized he was overmatched against a veteran attorney.

Roosevelt's opponent made a brilliant summary but argued the case at such length that he wore out the jurors' attention.

When it came his turn, Roosevelt addressed the jury with one simple argument: "Members of the jury, you have heard the evidence. You have also listened to my distinguished colleague, a brilliant orator. If you believe him and disbelieve the evidence, you will have to decide in his favor. That is all I have to say."

It was enough. Roosevelt won the case.

Columbia University Professor William Peterfield Trent offered this advice to students intending to become teachers: "It will frequently happen when you are holding forth that someone in the class will disagree. You will be tempted to go after him and convert him then and there. Don't do it. He is probably the only one who is listening."

LADIES, IF YOU'RE THINKING OF GOING FOR A
WALK IN A THUNDERSTORM, TAKE A GUY WITH
YOU. MEN ARE HIT BY LIGHTNING FOUR TIMES
AS OFTEN AS WOMEN.

What happens to sibling rivalry when one brother gets a major break in Hollywood and the other doesn't?

When Charlie Korsmo was cast at thirteen to star with Robin Williams in Steven Spielberg's *Hook*, his older brother told him he could have done the role better.

"I would have punched him," Charlie said, "but he's bigger than I am. He just hit his growth spurt. I should have punched him last year."

"**Y**ou learn to steer your way around your own shortcomings," physicist Steven Toulmin said. "The world is made up of getting a little better at things."

"**S**hoot the brave officers," General Stonewall Jackson advised his troops during the Civil War. "The cowards will run away and take their men with them."

What do the people in charge think of the rest of us? Not much. But they're happy to take our money anyway.

Take something as innocent as a trip to the candy counter at your local megaplex. Perhaps tonight you'd enjoy a Charleston Chew or box of Jujubes with the movie. But you can't find those brands, and you don't like any of the dozen choices offered.

Why won't movie theaters offer a wider selection of treats? They could. They choose not to, because they don't think you can handle it.

Theater owners have such a low opinion of movie-goers, they figure you'll stand at the counter with a dumb look on your face, unable to make up your little mind and holding up the line.

In the candy racket, move-through is all. Head 'em up, move 'em out, jelly beans. Theater owners want you to settle for what you can get and move on, so people at the back of the line don't give up and go watch a movie without stuffing their faces.

Movie theaters depend on soda, popcorn, and candy sales for their profits. The movie studios get nearly all of the outrageous sum you pay for the tickets. As far as studios are concerned, candy and soda are pacifiers that make bad movies not so dreadful.

Movie mogul Harry Cohn knew how to tell if a film was any good: "If my fanny squirms, it's bad. If my fanny doesn't squirm, it's good."

TWO

THE ENDLESS KISS AND OTHER ODD ACCOMPLISHMENTS OF ORDINARY PEOPLE

As a stunt for Ricki Lake's TV show in 2001, a couple kissed for thirty-one hours.

As they were kissing through that fifth hour, it must have occurred to them: Why are we doing this?

In the ninth hour, I'll bet they were asking themselves: Do I ever want to see this person ever again, ever?

From hour nineteen through hour twenty-five they were just

plain stubborn. But somewhere in the punch-drunk thirtieth hour, they must have thought: Is there a planet in this universe where people won't do incredibly stupid things just to get on TV?

And the answer must have come to them: certainly not this one.

A different kind of oral exhibitionism went on at an Illinois summer camp in 2001, when 297 people lined up and used a single string of dental floss (1,500 feet long) to floss their teeth simultaneously.

IN 1990 A TEAM OF TEN BRITISH ROYAL MARINES PUSHED A LARGE BABY CARRIAGE IN WHICH AN ADULT SAT DRESSED LIKE A BABY FOR 271.7 MILES IN TWENTY-FOUR HOURS.

Hollywood producers spend millions and use the latest in computer tools to create the amazing SFX that enliven their movies. But sometimes the most impressive special effects are the simplest and the cheapest.

Makeup artist Jack Pierce helped actor Boris Karloff create the monster for the classic 1931 film, *Frankenstein*. The monster's giant head was a rubber mask, and Karloff was aided in that stiff-legged walk by wearing two pairs of pants with steel strut inserts.

Those extra-long arms, whose reach frightened kids for years? That was achieved through real Hollywood magic. To make the monster's arms look longer on camera, Pierce simply shortened the sleeves of Karloff's coat.

Backward racing is a little-seen specialty among distance athletes. Anthony Thornton of Minneapolis spent New Year's Eve of 1988 walking backward for twenty-four hours. He covered 95.4 miles.

In 1994 Timothy Badyna ran the Toledo, Ohio, marathon backward, covering the twenty-six–plus miles in under four hours, faster than most people could do it moving forward.

Toothpick carver Bob Shamey of Ligonier, Pennsylvania, carved a single toothpick into a chain seventeen links long to celebrate his birthday on April 18, 1993.

Then there are the stunts that make you wonder how anyone thought them up. In 1930 a teenager named Johnny Pearce swam for two and a half miles while smoking a pipe without letting the tobacco go out.

Forty old-time baseball pitchers have accomplished an amazing feat that no modern pitcher will ever duplicate: pitching and winning both games of a doubleheader while going the distance in each game. No one's done it since 1926, and the way pitchers are now handled, no one will do it again.

Even more amazing: Joe McGinnity, who pitched for the New York Giants, won both games of a doubleheader three times—all during the month of August 1903.

There will always be librarians: In Victorian England, before Dewey and his decimal system took over book arrangements, it was considered indecent for a book written by a woman to be placed on a shelf next to a book written by a man—unless the authors were married to each other.

Meanwhile, the University of Cambridge created a special library section for books written by lunatics and morons. How these librarians determined which writers were lunatics is lost to history.

The morons may have been a little easier to identify. For example, these books might have qualified:

1) In seventeenth-century France, an anonymous enemy of the Duke d'Epernon published a five-hundred-page book called *The Exploits of the Duke d'Epernon*. Every page in the book was blank.

2) In 1969 experimental writer José Luis Castillejo published a book that contained nothing but the letter "i" printed in random pat-

terns on page after page. The writer conceived the book as a protest against the "tyranny of words we call literature."

3) Timothy Dexter, an eighteenth-century merchant, published his autobiography without using a single mark of punctuation. Then on the last page, he printed line after line of periods, commas, exclamation points, and question marks.

  Dexter instructed readers to "peper and solt (the book) as they plese." Spelling wasn't a big issue with Dexter either.

4) In 1561 a book called *Missae ac Missalis Anatomia* was published, containing fifteen pages of errata. The whole book ran to only 172 pages of text, setting a world record that has yet to be topped for really bad proofreading.

Must have seemed like a dream that day in 1973 when the people of Bydgoszcz, Poland, found beer pouring from their kitchen faucets instead of water. Like all dreams, it didn't last.

A breakdown at the town brewery had directed the beer away from the kegs and into the city's water lines. Someone fixed it. They never caught him.

In 1874 a patriotic American composer set the entire United States Constitution to music. In concert, the Constitution lasted six hours. The lyrics we still have, but the score has been lost to history.

Baseball players suit up and hit the field just about every day during the long season. But that still leaves too much free time for some of them to get into trouble.

On an off day, Joe "Mule" Sprinz, who played for the Cleveland Indians in 1931, bet that he could catch a ball thrown from a blimp. And he did. After packing his catcher's mitt with extra stuffing, the Mule caught a ball dropped from a blimp hovering eight hundred feet overhead.

What Sprinz wasn't ready for was the shockwave produced by the catch. It broke his jaw. He held onto the ball, though.

Newspaper columnist Marilyn vos Savant entertains and challenges readers with her high-IQ answers to their questions. In 1998 she published a list of odd questions she had received from readers over the years that were unanswerable—or that she "loved too much" to answer. Here are a few beauts:

1) Has all this evolution been worth it?

2) How can a deodorant have a scent of its own? Why doesn't it wipe itself out?

3) Could we stop a hurricane if everyone on the East Coast pointed their fans east?

4) When I throw my underpants into the washer, they come back inside out. But if I put them in inside out, they still come back inside out. Can you explain this?

5) Is there an implied time limit on fortune cookie predictions? If so, how long is it?

Horace Fletcher, a health-food faddist in the early 1900s, advocated chewing your food seventy times before swallowing. "Nature will castigate those who don't masticate," he warned, thus creating one of the all-time worst slogans.

All around the country, Fletcherites could be identified at dinner parties and in restaurants by their obsessive chewing and the fact that everyone else was finished with their meal while they had barely begun.

> IN HIS FIRST AT BAT, CHICAGO CUBS CATCHER CUNO BARRAGAN HIT BOTH HIS FIRST AND HIS LAST HOME RUN IN THE MAJORS.

Detroit Tigers catcher Harry Chiti became the only player in baseball history to get traded for himself.

The Tigers traded Chiti to the New York Mets for that ever-popular player to be named later. When he arrived in New York, the Mets decided they didn't want him after all. So they named him later and shipped him back to Detroit.

Belle Boyd, born into a wealthy Virginia family, became infamous during the Civil War as an audacious spy for the Confederacy. When captured by the Union Army, she charmed her captors into releasing her, and then went back to spying for the South.

Belle so won over one Union officer that he helped her escape from his own custody. He was arrested; she fled. They were reunited and married in England.

As a girl, Belle showed an early aptitude for flaunting convention. When her parents sent her from the room because, at eleven, she was too young to join one of their elegant dinner parties, Belle shocked the guests by riding her horse into the dining room.

"My horse is old enough, isn't he?" the girl demanded.

Belle wasn't the only audacious kid who liked to ride her horse where horses weren't meant to go. How about the kids who snuck their ponies on the elevator up to the second floor of the White House? That would be President Teddy Roosevelt's kids.

When frontiersman Davy Crockett served in Congress, he introduced a reasonable motion that the House of Representatives serve whiskey for free to its members.

"Congress allows lemonade to members, and it is charged under the head of stationery," Crockett argued. "I move that whiskey be allowed under the item of fuel."

You can become infamous not for what you do but for surviving what you do — or what gets done to you.

1)   A French woman was confused when her bad headaches lasted for a week. When she could stand the pain no longer, she went to a doctor. He found the source of her headaches: while she'd been asleep, her husband had shot her in the head.

It's rare, but it does happen, that people can be shot and not notice and not suffer severe effects.

Once the doctor discovered the bullet wound, the woman's husband was arrested.

2)   In 1927 a woman checked into the Ontario Hospital in Canada complaining of abdominal pains. The doctors operated and removed two thousand objects she had swallowed, including one thousand pins.

Dustin Hoffman had his first hit movie with *The Graduate*, winning the hearts of young America by running off with the bride on her wedding day. Everyone who saw the movie remembers the vision of Katherine Ross in her white wedding dress running with her beloved for the bus through the streets of Berkeley.

Mike Nichols, who directed *The Graduate*, imagined what would have happened if Katherine and Dustin had run off like that in real life. "They ride on for another five minutes," Nichols conjectured, "then she says, 'I haven't a thing to wear.'"

During a summer break, a music student from an American college toured Germany and visited Beethoven's home in Bonn, which had been turned into a museum.

She stood at the ropes, staring at the piano upon which Beethoven had once composed his glorious music. When other visitors moved on, the student offered the guard a bribe if he would allow her to play Beethoven's piano.

The guard agreed, and the girl played her favorite Beethoven composition. Afterward, she said, "I imagine many of the great pianists who have visited here have played on this piano."

"No," the guard said. "Paderewski was here last year, but he said he was not worthy to touch it."

THREE

BIZARRE BREAKDOWNS: RARE OCCASIONS WHEN THINGS THAT SHOULD WORK DON'T

When the Coca-Cola Company introduced Coke to China in the 1920s, it used Chinese characters that when spoken would sound out "Coca-Cola." What the marketing execs didn't quite grasp was the meaning behind the sounds.

The characters they chose did not mean "flavored fizzy water" or "something to drink," but "bite the wax tadpole."

No one knows: perhaps things do go better when you bite the wax tadpole.

We're not surprised when the car breaks down, or the air conditioner, or the government. But there are things we've grown accustomed to counting on: Coke not reminding us of wax tadpoles, speakers being audible, and brownnosing the boss being an effective career strategy. When these basics break down, the world gets weird.

The business strategy of kissing up to the boss is popular because it's proven so effective. When did this approach last go wrong? We have to go back a hundred years.

Alfred Northcliffe was a newspaper publisher who founded the *London Daily Mail* in 1896. He was rough on reporters. He once cornered his staff and asked if they were happy working for him.

"Yes, sir," a quick-witted reporter responded, knowing it's smart to be at the head of the line of people kissing up to the boss.

Northcliffe immediately fired that writer, explaining, "I don't want anyone here to be content on five pounds a week."

Kings, down through the ages, have found an effective method of dealing with people who oppose them, displease them or wear the wrong color shirt on a day when the king gets up on the wrong side of the throne—off with their heads!

Then there was King Louis XI of France, who bungled the simplest and most effective of commands. The king maneuvered himself into a situation where, as the most powerful person in the land, he didn't dare attack a commoner who had no army, no political power, nothing but his wits to keep his head.

Like many people in the fifteenth century, King Louis accepted astrology as a science, as accurate as any other of the rudimentary sciences of his time. The king felt threatened by one court astrologer who was too accurate in his predictions. Louis decided it would be safer to have him murdered then risk his growing influence in court.

Louis made one mistake—he wanted to humiliate his victim first so the astrologer would realize he didn't know as much as he thought he did before he went under the assassin's knife.

Before signaling his guards to move in for the kill, Louis asked the astrologer, "Tell me what your own fate will be? How long do you have to live?"

The astrologer calmly replied, "I shall die just three days before Your Majesty."

The king didn't dare take the chance that the prediction would prove accurate. The astrologer walked away from certain death thanking his lucky stars.

Since the police tend to catch only the dumb or unlucky crooks, burglary is one of the more profitable of the criminal professions. Not as rewarding as politics, perhaps; but if burglars aren't caught in the act, they're seldom caught at all, and stolen goods are rarely recovered. Rarer still is what happened to the Scottish poet James Montgomery.

The poet had many valuable items stolen from his home in 1812. One of them, a treasured desk, was returned with this note from a member of the burglary gang: "Honored sir: When we robbed your house, we did not know that you wrote such beautiful verses as you do. I send this desk back. It was my share of the booty, and I hope you and God will forgive me."

As pro football linemen get larger, height becomes a major issue for the quarterbacks, who have to see over the charge to throw passes. Although quarterback Cade McNown stood six-foot-one when drafted by the Chicago Bears in 1999, some football commentators said he was too short to play in the NFL.

Bears' offensive coordinator Gary Crownton defended his hope for the future, telling reporters, "He's about the size of a lot of guys that size."

The Bears gave up on McNown two years later.

Does Hollywood suffer from Double-Standard Syndrome? Dr. Ricki Pollycove of California thought so and sent condoms to movie studio execs.

While stars, producers, and directors crusade against AIDS in their off-screen lives, movie studios continue to "make films in which sex scenes show no use of protection or even imply it," Dr. Pollycove said.

If filmmakers weren't willing to show couples using protection, Dr. Pollycove suggested the studios run this on-screen disclaimer: "Although the use of protection in sex scenes featured in this film is not shown, it should not be construed in any way as a reflection of how to conduct your sex life."

Why stop there? Action movies could run this disclaimer: "Although the star in this movie appears to be bulletproof, this should not be construed in any way as a reflection of how to stay alive."

In 1910 curators at the Louvre in Paris put the museum's most famous paintings, including the Mona Lisa, behind glass to protect them. This caution affronted French art lovers.

To protest the absurdity of glassing great art, the writer Roland Dorgeles took a razor into the museum and shaved in the reflection provided by a distorted Rembrandt.

The Mona Lisa was stolen in 1911 by an Italian patriot determined to return the painting to the country where it was created. Two years later, the thief was caught, and the undamaged painting returned to the Louvre.

Many people have a paralyzing fear of making speeches in public. They devise strange methods to overcome that fear.

1) English Prime Minister Winston Churchill eventually became

one of the most inspirational orators in history. He overcame his initial fear of public speaking by imagining that everyone in the audience had holes in their socks.

2) The writer Christopher Morley misplaced his glasses before giving a speech. As he gazed tentatively over the audience, he spotted in the second row "a most gorgeously furred-up woman," he recalled. "I thought: That's my audience. She fairly drips fur."

As he lectured, Morley never took his eyes off the woman, and he was pleased to notice that she was fascinated by his talk, never budging an inch as he spoke.

Afterward, a friend asked Morley, "Why did you keep staring at that chair in the second row?" It was the chair where the women had all piled their coats.

3) Matthew Arnold, the nineteenth-century English poet, hoped to supplement his meager income by giving lectures—a strange decision considering his dread fear of public speaking. Faced with an audience, Arnold talked in a whisper, so softly no one could hear him.

Arnold pressed on, arranging a tour of America, giving dozens of lectures to people who could not understand a word he said.

Fear of public speaking is common. One simple solution: Don't speak in public.

A politician challenged the French writer Alexandre Dumas to a duel. Both men were crack shots, so they decided on a novel approach: they would draw lots, and the loser would shoot himself. Dumas lost the draw.

Taking his pistol into his room, the author shut the door behind him. The witnesses waited tensely until they heard the shot, then rushed to the door. They found Dumas smoking a cigar, the revolver in his hand. "Gentlemen," he announced with a shrug, "a most regrettable thing has happened—I missed!"

When the first cars took to the roads of Pennsylvania in the late 1800s, the Farmers' Anti-Automobile Society petitioned the state government to protect horse riders by adopting sensible rules of the road.

The rules demanded that when a horse-drawn wagon approached, an auto driver had to cover his car with a blanket until the horses had safely passed. If the horses were unnerved by the car, the driver had to dismantle his car and hide it in the bushes until the wagon was gone.

Last time we drove through Pennsylvania, it appeared those rules were no longer being enforced.

Sometimes you can get something so right you don't believe it—and neither does anyone else.

In 1952 the computer was an unproven gizmo used only by engineers. Most people considered computers dubious science fiction.

The Remington Rand Company, which developed the '50s' most advanced computer, proposed to CBS TV that its UNIVAC mainframe could predict the winner of the presidential election based on exit polls.

Early on election night, UNIVAC predicted that General Dwight Eisenhower would defeat Adlai Stevenson in a landslide. But the Remington Rand engineers pleaded with CBS not to go on air with that prediction.

Why did the computer experts chicken out? Because all the political experts had predicted a very close race. The engineers figured something had gone wrong with UNIVAC and didn't want to look like fools the day after the election.

Turned out all the pundits were wrong. The computer called it right: Eisenhower in a landslide.

After heavyweight champ John L. Sullivan retired from the ring, he was asked for boxing lessons by a young man who, after one round, regretted the request. Sullivan didn't pull his punches, and the overmatched student couldn't get out of the ring fast enough.

"Mr. Sullivan, it was my idea to learn enough from you to be able to lick a certain guy I've got it in for," the student explained when he recovered from the pounding. "But I've changed my mind. I'll just send this fellow down here to take the rest of my lessons for me."

Politicians have big mouths, we know, but big buttered feet? Here's British Foreign Minister Ernest Bevin saying a mouthful: "If you let that sort of thing go on, your bread and butter will be cut right out from under your feet."

No word from Bevin on what his bread and butter was doing under his feet to begin with.

Looking for good advice you can never use? Listen to golfer Lee Trevino on how to avoid getting hit by lightning if you're overtaken by a storm on the links.

Move to the middle of the fairway, Trevino advised, and hold a one-iron over your head. "Not even God can hit a one-iron," he explained.

Baseball star Yogi Berra pointed out the twisted truth of popularity when he said, "Anyone who is popular is bound to be disliked."

"I went to a bookstore and asked the clerk for the self-help section," comic Brian Kiley joked. "She said, 'If I told you, that would defeat the whole purpose.'"

NEWSPAPER COLUMNIST JIMMY BRESLIN: "WHEN YOU STOP DRINKING, YOU HAVE TO DEAL WITH THIS MARVELOUS PERSONALITY THAT STARTED YOU DRINKING IN THE FIRST PLACE."

British Prime Minister Margaret Thatcher: "I always cheer up immensely if an attack is particularly wounding, because I think: well, if they attack one personally, it means they have not a single political argument left."

Only one man in the world had this problem—and he was the only person who couldn't solve it.

"It often happens that I wake at night and begin to think about a serious problem and decide I must tell the pope about it," Pope John XXIII reported. "Then I wake up completely and remember I am the pope."

William the Conqueror sailed across the channel from France and successfully invaded England in 1066. He decreed that French would be the official language of his new domain.

Plans to turn the English into Frenchmen were defeated, but not in battle. Here's how the English prevailed: His soldiers married English girls. While their husbands were out fighting recalcitrant Brits, their wives taught their children to speak English instead of French.

That's why the English still speak English. Unfortunately, the English women also taught their children to cook like the English instead of the French. And that's why you should wait until you get to Paris to have dinner.

"The obscure we see eventually," TV newsman Edward R. Murrow said. "The completely apparent takes longer."

And the impossible we expect by five o'clock. Here are three people who created impossible situations for others to deal with:

1) Benjamin Jowett, a nineteenth-century Oxford scholar, had an offbeat way of keeping students out of his hair so he could devote time to his own studies.

A student who was having trouble with his research complained to Jowett that he had searched through philosophical treatises both ancient and modern but had found no evidence of God.

Jowett could see a long debate looming ahead of him. He cut it short by instructing the shocked student, "If you don't find a God by five o'clock this afternoon, you must leave this college."

2) Readers of serious literature struggle with the density and referential obscurity of the long, thick novels by Irish writer James Joyce.

When asked why his writing was so difficult, Joyce shrugged it off. "The demand I make of my reader," he said, "is that he should devote his whole life to reading my works."

3) Mary Livermore was a nineteenth-century campaigner for the rights of women. While still in her teens, she led a group of girls who petitioned the president of Harvard University to reverse the school's men-only policy.

When Harvard authorities refused to allow women into classes, Livermore surprised them with a strange condemnation: "I wish I were God, that I might kill every woman from Eve down and let you have the masculine world all to yourselves and see how you would like that."

That kind of insightful thinking should have qualified her not just for studying at Harvard, but for teaching there.

A study at the University of California, Irvine, showed that IQ scores improved from listening to Mozart. Unfortunately, the improvements only lasted a few minutes.

Weird star names? How about all of them?

Astronomers down through the centuries have given newly identified stars names that drive students crazy trying to memorize and spell them. They follow this procedure because when the astronomers were in school, their teachers drove them crazy, making them memorize unmemorable names. The urge to pass it on motivates scientific traditions.

This is how we get stars with such suffering-student names as: Sadalmelik, Beta Camelopardalis, Alpha Chamaeleontis, Phakt, Kitalpha, Alpha Horologii, Praecipua, Zubeneschamali, Unukalhai, and Rasalhague.

A few stars were named by the fun astronomers: Zeta Puppis, Alpha Scuti, Alpha Pyxidis, and Alpha Telescopium.

The ancient Chinese Emperor Shih Huang Ti ordered all the books in his kingdom burned. Anyone caught hiding a manuscript was executed. Shih reasoned that since he was the mightiest of all emperors, history should start all over again from his reign.

To foil the emperor, Chinese poets, philosophers, and followers of Confucius memorized their favorite texts before turning the manuscripts over to the bonfires of the book burners.

Centuries later, another advocate of keeping people in the dark, General William Westmoreland, said, "Without censorship, things can get terribly confused in the public mind." But not in the general's, obviously.

Censorship always clashes with our curious natures. As soon as people learn you don't want them to know something, that's all they want to know.

> "BEFORE I GOT MARRIED, I HAD SIX THEORIES
> ABOUT BRINGING UP CHILDREN," LORD
> ROCHESTER SAID. "NOW I HAVE SIX CHILDREN
> AND NO THEORIES."

Londoners in the seventeenth century were outraged by a new fashion trend, worried it would weaken the stout blood of the true Englishman: umbrellas.

One anti-umbrella-ist petitioned the government to have the devices banned, arguing, "The purpose of rain is to make people wet."

According to the nineteenth-century hygiene expert Dr. Dio Lewis, women should avoid all salt, pepper, ketchup, mustard, and Worcestershire sauce. Why?

Consuming them would make women promiscuous. "Everything which inflames one appetite is likely to arouse the other also," Dr. Lewis explained.

This may explain why some people shake so much salt on their food or smother it with ketchup. Cheaper than Viagra.

FOUR

ANCIENT WRISTWATCHES: WHAT WERE THEY THINKING— IF AT ALL?

In 1999 two teenage shoplifters were caught after they stole food from a San Diego mini-mart, and then returned to the store a few minutes later. Why did they go back? To ask the clerk for a bag to put their stolen food in.

What were they thinking? Or had they moved beyond the need to think? Many happy people don't think at all, and they're still richer than you.

Wilson Mizner was a legendary con man of the 1920s. He grew rich helping to redistribute the wealth by selling Florida swampland to foolish investors. One victim of a Mizner swindle took him to court. "Mizner said I'd be able to grow nuts, and I can't grow a thing because my land is under water," the man argued.

Mizner's defense? The plaintiff was hard of hearing. "I told him if he bought my property he would go nuts," Mizner claimed. "I think he already has." The judge dismissed the case.

"IN BOXING THEY HAVE THE UNDISPUTED HEAVYWEIGHT CHAMPION," COMIC GEORGE CARLIN OBSERVED. "IF IT'S UNDISPUTED, WHAT'S ALL THE FIGHTING ABOUT?"

A movie studio made a film version of the opera *Carmen* in 1915. It was a silent film.

Here's a contest that no single government official could have come up with alone. This idea required the clear thinking and decision making of a government committee.

In 1974 the U.S. Army Materiel Command offered a prize of $100 to whoever came up with the best name for the command's new headquarters building. There were five hundred entries in the contest. The winner: The AMC Building.

I don't know about you, but as a taxpayer I want my hundred bucks back.

Coordinating a big battle scene for a major motion picture, like Mel Gibson's *Braveheart*, is a monumental undertaking, as complicated as coordinating forces for a real-life military campaign — plus makeup.

Stars, supporting cast, the stunt crew, and hundreds of extras all require costumes, direction, and rehearsal so that everyone does the right thing at the right time and in the precise place to be captured by the cameras.

The director and the assistants must check thousands of details before the shooting starts. Then, action! Get it right and get it on camera.

Here's one little lesson they forgot during the production of *Braveheart*: Before you film a massive medieval battle, make sure all your ancient Scot warriors have taken off their sunglasses.

After the *Braveheart* crew shot the big battle scene, they looked at the film footage and saw that some of the extras were not only wearing sunglasses but also wristwatches. "Take two."

Can you imagine how much more painful this multiple brain freeze would have been if *Braveheart* hadn't turned into a box-office blockbuster?

In 1979, Austrian police locked a man in a jail cell, and then forgot they'd put him there. Eighteen days later, they remembered. The man, unable to shout loud enough to rouse help, survived without food or water for that long, but barely.

A South African marriage counselor found he couldn't help one bickering couple. They squabbled all the time. During a therapy session in 1999, the nagging wife kept criticizing her husband, finding fault with everything he did and said. The husband finally blew his stack, lurched out of his chair, and slapped her.

Right behind him came the counselor — lurching out of his chair. But instead of coming to the wife's rescue, the counselor slapped her too.

"She's the most annoying woman I've ever been around," the counselor said, trying to explain his outburst. "No husband should be subjected to nagging like that."

In 1921, U.S. General Billy Mitchell took on the military and political establishments in Washington by insisting that America had to prepare for an air war, that planes would soon be capable of sinking battleships in naval battles.

The military experts didn't believe him. In the early days of the airplane, nearly everyone (but Mitchell) could see the obvious: that planes would never be advanced enough to become an important weapon of war.

Mitchell insisted he could demonstrate the superiority of air power. He proposed to have his planes attack an unmanned German battleship that the United States had captured during World War I.

Washington authorities laughed off Mitchell's claims. "That idea is so damned nonsensical and impossible that I'm willing to stand on the bridge of the battleship," claimed Newton Baker, who was secretary of war in 1921, "while that nitwit tries to hit it from the air."

Baker was lucky General Mitchell didn't take him up on the dare. In July of that year, Mitchell was finally given the OK to demonstrate his attack planes. They sank the battleship in minutes.

At the 1995 Oscar ceremony, the stars were slowly making their way down the crowded red carpet as photographers pressed against the ropes to take their pictures, and fans screamed their heads off.

Caught up in the thrill of it all, a gushy TV interviewer spotted comic actor Steve Martin inching toward her through the star jam. Clutching her microphone, she shouted at him, "You must be really, really thrilled to be here tonight at this truly, truly wonderful event, even though your film wasn't nominated, although it was actually, actually terrific."

At which point, Martin gave her a pained smile and said, "I can't hear a word you're saying." Lucky him.

Great art is only great if it survives. Some of the best creations look like trash when it comes time to clean up.

1) In the sixteenth century, Dr. Thomas Cooper labored for eight years gathering notes for a dictionary of the English language. The exertion had a debilitating effect on his health, worrying his wife. When he was out one day, she went into his study and burned the entire work to free him from his labors.

Dr. Cooper spent the next eight years re-creating the destroyed work.

2) In the nineteenth century, English historian Thomas Carlyle struggled for a year to write the first volume of his *History of the French Revolution*. Finally finished with his epic book, Carlyle gave his only manuscript to friend and mentor John Stuart Mill for commentary.

Mill's maid thought it was waste paper and used the manuscript to start a cooking fire. Carlyle had to write the book all over again by hand. "I feel like a man who has nearly killed himself accomplishing zero," he said.

3) Mexican painter Jose Orozco would destroy his own paintings if they displeased him. He got some unwanted help with that impulse when he traveled to the United States in 1917 to set up a major exhibit.

A Customs officer in Laredo, Texas, ordered that sixty of Orozco's paintings be destroyed, because it was illegal to bring "immoral" pictures into the country.

4) Erigena was one of the few enlightened scholars of the ninth century. "Reason and authority come alike from the one source of Divine Wisdom," he argued, a view that would be casually accepted today. In his time, the church didn't take kindly to such wild heresy and banned Erigena's writings.

Four centuries later, his thoughts were still considered heresy, so Pope Honorius III had his manuscripts burned as "hereditary depravity."

5) When the song "Travelin' Man" was offered to soul singer Sam Cooke, his manager threw it in a trash can, because he knew a loser when he heard one. An assistant at the record company picked the sheet music out of the trash and gave it to pop star Ricky Nelson, who turned *Travelin' Man* into a No. 1 hit.

In 1929, Soviet leaders decided to bury the capitalist calendar propagated by the decadent West. The Communist regime forced the entire country to shift to a five-day week, with everyone working four days on the job and taking one day off.

Each day was given a color. Instead of waking up on Monday, you greeted the people's glorious new morning on Yellow, followed by the revolutionary days of Orange, Red, Purple, and Green.

To make sure all jobs were covered throughout the week, each person was color-coded for their day off. All Purples were off on Purple, all Oranges on Orange.

What the Soviet rulers created was calendar mud. If you were an Orange trying to date a Red, forget it. You'd never see each other.

By 1940 the Soviet Union gave up and rejoined the rest of the world with the ordinary seven days of the week. That's why the Russians don't say TGIG: Thank God It's Green.

> AT WHITE HOUSE CHRISTMAS PARTIES, FIRST LADY ELEANOR ROOSEVELT TREATED GUESTS TO A DINNER OF SAUSAGES, RAW ONIONS, AND SCRAMBLED EGGS. "SHE GETS ALL THESE ROMANTIC YOUNG COUPLES TOGETHER," A GUEST COMPLAINED, "THEN TRIES TO KILL THE ROMANCE."

The U.S. Department of Agriculture once paid for a study to find out whether American mothers preferred kids' clothes made of no-iron fabrics or fabrics that required ironing. Inquiring minds found out that, given the choice, moms would rather not iron their kids' clothes.

Actually, the Department of Agriculture didn't pay for the study. American taxpayers did. But it only cost us $100,000 to find out what anyone with a kid who wore clothes could have told them for nothing.

Coca-Cola instructed the company's advertising agency, in 1938, to follow these guidelines when promoting its soda:

1)   Be inclined to show a brunette rather than a blonde girl, if only one girl is in the picture.

2)   Never refer to Coca-Cola as "it."

3)   Never use Coca-Cola in a personal sense, such as "Coca-Cola invites you to lunch."

And here's the big one folks:

4)   Never infer that Coca-Cola should be bought by phone.

"Hi, can you send over a medium Coke, light on the ice? Half an hour? OK. $2.98, plus a $15 delivery charge? Got it."

When the U.S. Army sent soldiers to private colleges to study engineering, the bureaucrats assigned students to various schools in alphabetical order. That's how 298 of the 300 army students sent to one school were all named Brown.

What were they thinking? Not much if they're idiots. But it's not the morons we have to worry about. It's the geniuses.

It took the greatest collection of genius the United States could enlist to build the atomic bomb. Idiots couldn't blow up the world and wipe out the entire human race. Only the genius can get that job done.

Or as the comic Emo Philips put it, "Countries are making nuclear weapons like there's no tomorrow."

We remember Hippocrates as the Father of Medicine. Not so well known is his advice to women unhappy with the size of their busts, a problem that was of concern to women in ancient Greece and has been handed down through the ages.

Hippocrates told women they could increase the size of their bosoms by singing loudly every day. Odd that the Father of Medicine also invented the quack cure.

Eighteenth-century English astronomer Edmund Halley figured out that reports of three lights streaking across the sky seventy-five years apart were actually reappearances of the same comet. His remarkable leap to an unobvious conclusion turned out to be correct, and the comet was named after him.

But Halley also believed that the earth was hollow, and people lived inside.

So did John Cleves Symmes, an army officer who fought for America in the War of 1812. He spent years raising money for an expedition that would enter the hollow earth at the South Pole and emerge at the North Pole by walking through the empty middle.

Symmes reasoned that God would create hollow planets because he was frugal; solid planets were a waste of matter. The Lord would make planets hollow so people could live in the centers.

Symmes found support for his theory in Congress. Two ships set sail for the South Pole in 1829 to prove his theory correct. They were never heard from again.

President Richard Nixon was trying to protect himself from Watergate charges when he said, "When the president does it, that means it's not illegal." But he also offered plausible deniability to all the presidents to follow for their own dubious activities.

If nothing the president does is illegal, then why would anything he did be immoral? Does the two-party system permit the Republicans to have their illegalities, while the Democrats specialize in immoralities?

Who said: "If you've seen one slum, you've seen them all?" That would be the opinion of Vice President Spiro Agnew. Was he trying to make his boss, Richard Nixon, look good by comparison? Or had he actually seen all available slums so he knew what he was talking about?

Actually, Agnew was expressing the usually unspoken preference of most rich politicians—that if people are going to insist upon living in poverty, at least they can do it quietly.

"**G**aiety is the most outstanding feature of the Soviet Union." Who made that unique appraisal of the apparently humorless Soviet regime? Russian Premier Joseph Stalin.

Any Russian who was not gay enough was sent off to the gulags, where gaiety was enforced in Stalin's unique style.

"**W**hen future historians look back on our way of curing inflation," automaker Lee Iacocca predicted, "they'll probably compare it to bloodletting in the Middle Ages."

If they do, it will certainly add some excitement to the field of economic theory.

Ever think the users' guide that comes with your electronic gear is written by idiots? Apparently, that point is still open to debate. But it is necessary that users' manuals be written *for* idiots.

"I always tell my design students to write the explanations for the most stupid person you can think of," said Frederic Brunel, a professor of consumer design at Arizona State University. "You can't afford to have people miss it."

When is a gift not a gift? When it comes from Brian Hughes, a wealthy New York City businessman who donated land for a city park in the early 1900s.

When Brooklyn officials eagerly went to inspect their new park, they found that Hughes's land was exactly two feet wide and eight feet long. He had invented a park for one skinny person at a time.

Does anyone ask dumber questions than newspaper reporters? Sure, TV reporters.

When Diane Sawyer was a news anchor for ABC, she interviewed a butcher who'd been chosen to make Polish sausage for the pope. Sawyer, seeing a chance for redemption that the Bible failed to cover, asked the butcher, "Do you think the pope liking your sausage gets you a special place in heaven?"

"I was asked to come to Chicago," movie star Raquel Welch explained, "because Chicago is one of our fifty-two states."

Everyone enjoys a really stupid product warning label. But before you dismiss the manufacturers' lawyers as idiots, remember that the reason they put these warnings on their products is because someone did what they warn us against.

1) On a barbecue grill: "Do not touch coals to see if the charcoal is hot."

2) A special warning to brides from Emily Post: "While wearing your wedding veil, remember not to smoke."

3) On the army's claymore mines: "Front, toward enemy."

4) On a bottle of sleeping pills: "Warning: May cause drowsiness."

5) On a hair dryer: "Do not use while sleeping."

6) On Christmas lights: "For indoor or outdoor use only."

7) For an iron: "Do not iron clothes on body."

8) On a pudding package: "Product will be hot after heating." Let us hope so.

FIVE

THE MAN WITHOUT A PENCIL: UNUSUAL PEOPLE AND THEIR BIZARRE TALENTS

Sinking forty-six balls in a row? Plenty of pool sharks can do it. But Henry Lewis, a billiards master from the 1920s, ran forty-six in a row without using a cue stick. What did he use instead? His nose.

Which leads us to the question: Do eccentrics also have odd talents—or do odd talents make them eccentric?

Ronald Knox was an Oxford scholar known for his keen, if eccentric, mind. One day while traveling by train with a friend, he opened the *London Times* and spent the first part of the ride staring blankly at the crossword puzzle without writing in a single answer.

The *Times'* puzzles were considered the most difficult, and Knox was getting nowhere with it. His friend noticed that Knox had no pencil and offered to lend him one so he could fill in the puzzle.

"No thanks," Knox replied, "just finished."

Napoleon was known not only for his military genius but also for his ability to work on affairs of state hour after hour, long after his subordinates would tire and retire for the night.

One of Napoleon's followers exclaimed in praise, "God made Bonaparte and then rested."

An overworked assistant had a different view: "God should have rested a little earlier."

Before he became a movie star in the 1920s, W. C. Fields got his start in showbiz as a juggler. Fields understood that audiences didn't know enough to appreciate the skill of master jugglers working with balls and clubs. So he practiced sixteen hours a day to master his skills at juggling cigars, eggs, biscuits, canes, and frying pans.

Handy people:

1) William Dampier was a nineteenth-century artist whose hands were paralyzed, so he wrote and illustrated books by holding a pen between his teeth.

2) The switch-hitters:

Swiss artist Paul Klee painted with his left hand but wrote with his right.

President James Madison sometimes wrote with his left, sometimes with his right.

Leonardo da Vinci could draw with one hand while writing with the other.

President James Garfield wrote Greek with one hand while writing Latin with the other.

3) A Chinese artist of the 1920s, Huang Erhnan, specialized in silk paintings using a unique brush: his tongue.

4) The French mathematician Jean-Victor Poncelet was forced to fight in Napoleon's army in the disastrous invasion of Russia. Captured by the Russians, he was locked in a prison for two years.

Without paper or writing instruments, Poncelet put his imprisonment to use, solving math problems. He scratched formulae on the walls of his cell with pebbles, solving all the axioms of projective geometry.

Tom Wiggins from Georgia could copy anything on the piano after hearing it only once and without needing to practice. In the nineteenth century, he toured Europe showing off his amazing talent.

Cardinal Giuseppe Mezzofanti of Italy had a unique talent for learning languages, speaking eighty-eight languages and dialects fluently, including Algonquin, Chippewa, Walachian, and Frisian. His linguistic ability was all the more remarkable considering that the cardinal never left Italy.

Although speed-painting and sprint-poetry have yet to achieve wide popularity, the standards in these fields were set by the same man, the Indian mystic Sri Chinmoy.

In 1975 he finished 16,031 paintings in a single day. Then he composed 843 poems in twenty-four hours.

Why sprint-poetry is so much more time-consuming than speed-painting remains unclear.

Master violinist Nicolo Paganini would show off his virtuosity by performing on a single-stringed violin. Or he would fray a string of his regular violin so it would snap during a concert. Then he could impress the audience by continuing, without missing a note, on the surviving strings.

Paganini made a fortune performing throughout Europe but lost it all in the casinos. For all his talents, Paganini could not solve this riddle: If wealthy gamblers already have a fortune, why risk losing it to get another one?

Vaudeville was the great Theater of Yes, a surprisingly democratic form of entertainment. With a dozen or more acts in a show, if you had almost any kind of talent you could find a vaudeville theater in which to perform.

Only vaudeville would have found room for an act as unusual as Sadakichi Hartman, the perfumist. He came on stage with his fans and blew a concert of perfumes out over the audience.

In 2001 Luis Silva of Portugal kept a tennis ball bouncing in the air by hitting it with his head for fifty-nine minutes and fifty-three seconds, to set a world record in an event most people didn't even know was an event.

In 1972 John Sebastian, an Illinois high school basketball player, made sixty-three free throws in a row while blindfolded.

In 1971 English seamstress Brenda Robinson set a record for needle-threading: 3,795 threads through 3,795 needles in two hours.

King Bran, according to the early British historian Geoffrey of Monmouth, ruled the British Isles in the years before the Romans conquered the land. As a king, Bran had one unique characteristic: his head had been chopped off. But according to the legend he continued to rule without any problems for eighty years.

We know why the numerical length of pi torments high school math students. But why does it compel the obsessive?

Hans Eberstar, a man with an amazing memory, put on a demonstration at George Washington University in 1988, proving to the assembled mathematicians that he could recite pi to the 11,944th place.

Many musicians have extraordinary memories. Few approach the mastery of musical memory shown by composer Arturo Toscanini. As a young cellist, Toscanini played an adagio by Bozoni in a string quartet. The four players met up a year later and wanted to play the composition again, but no one had the score.

Toscanini grabbed some paper and wrote, from memory, all four parts of the adagio.

Film director Orson Welles was surprised by the small turnout for one of his lectures. He introduced himself to the few people in the audience by listing his credits as a Hollywood writer, actor, director, and producer.

Welles went on to mention his many other talents: that he wrote and directed for the theater and radio shows; that he was a painter and a magician; and that he could play piano and violin.

"Isn't it a pity," he concluded, "that there are so many of me and so few of you."

In the 1900s many circuses featured bears trained to ride bicycles. Did you know that bears also learn to jump rope, walk a tightrope, tumble on a trampoline, and juggle?

Bears, in general, are so smart, strong, and unchallenged that they have only one major problem—people.

In the sixteenth century, the dubious cat organ enjoyed a brief popularity. This was a large box, divided into compartments, each of which had a hole in the bottom. Cats were put inside the box with their tails sticking out through the holes. To play the music of squealing cats, the organist yanked on their tails.

An even odder form of music: the pig organ. A fifteenth-century musician arranged a herd of pigs under cover, and then attached spikes to a keyboard so he could play squeal-tunes for the amusement of King Louis XI of France.

IN INDIA A UNIVERSITY PROFESSOR TRAINED RATS TO DO YOGA. WHILE OTHER INVENTORS WORKED ON BUILDING A BETTER MOUSETRAP, HE BUILT A BETTER MOUSE.

The French acrobat Charles Blondin was the greatest tightrope walker of the nineteenth century. He took to the wire at age six and then moved his act out of the circus tent into the great and dangerous outdoors, where no nets were possible.

Blondin became famous for mastering Niagara Falls on a wire, where a slip would have meant spectacular death. Over the years, he crossed the falls (1,300 feet on a rope) many times in a variety of bizarre ways: on stilts, in a sack, with his hands and feet tied, pushing a wheelbarrow, and carrying a man on his back.

Amazingly, Blondin continued performing into his seventies. He beat the odds by dying in bed.

Blondin knew what he was risking and what he could do. But there's another kind of amazing talent—the accidental, when someone pulls the most unlikely fat out of the fire.

Parachutes were primitive in 1908, but a troupe of performers dazzled crowds by parachuting out of hot air balloons.

One woman in the troupe, Louise May, faced certain death when her parachute failed to open after she jumped out of a balloon at eleven thousand feet. Another diver, Dolly Shepherd, caught Louise on her way down. Both women descended safely on a single chute.

They do this all the time in the movies. Not so often in real life.

Sometimes a person's talent is making surprising use of a lack of talent. That's how Harpo Marx broke into showbiz.

Before the Marx Brothers became a hot comedy act on the vaudeville circuit, Harpo landed a job playing piano in theaters to accompany silent movies.

Harpo's problem: he only knew one song on the piano. So he played it fast for the action scenes and slowly for the love scenes.

You can't totally script a news anchor like Dan Rather—no matter how much CBS wanted to at times. Rather had an odd way of expressing himself when the news excited him. Here are three rather odd Ratherisms:

1) "Frankly, we don't know whether to run, to watch, or to bark at the moon."

2) "Sip it, savor it, cup it, photostat it, underline it in red, put it in an album, hang it on the wall: George Bush is the next president of the United States."

3) "When the going gets weird, anchormen punt."

An Arizona man developed one of those hobbies that are extremely difficult and utterly useless: crafting giant, non-functional knives. His crowning achievement: a twenty-seven-pound folding knife with four blades. The knife was ten feet long and of no use to anyone but trivia fans.

Chess master Wilhelm Steinitz became convinced he could move chess pieces around the board without touching them. The fact that he couldn't do it didn't convince him otherwise. He also believed he could make phone calls without using a telephone.

Steinitz once challenged God to a game of chess and, to make it interesting, offered him a pawn handicap.

Even if you're not particularly talented, you have some amazing talents. For example, most of us can look at millions of different colors and shades and recognize their subtle differences.

All of us can create movies that are more imaginative and meaningful than anything created by the best Hollywood filmmakers—and we do it without actors, director, budget, or effort—just about every night of the week.

And whining! We are the whine masters of creation. No matter how bad or good things are, the complaining never stops.

SIX

$7 MILLION FOR CATS AND OTHER ODD WAYS TO GET RID OF MONEY

Diamond Jim Brady was king of the high life in the early 1900s. He made a fortune and spent it on food, fun, and all that glittered. On his New Jersey dairy farm, Brady's cows were milked into gold pails.

Brady loaned large sums of money to friends and associates. Before he died in 1917, Brady took IOUs totaling half a million dollars and tore them up, explaining, "I'm not going to leave trouble and heartache behind me."

Few rich people have that kind of class. Few classy people have that kind of money. Fortunately for our amusement, money tends to get people twisted up in curious ways.

In 2004 a Hong Kong man, desperate to become a pro basketball player, paid $2,600 to a beauty salon that promised to make him taller.

He was five-foot-nine. Anyone seen any new Hong Kong players coming into the NBA standing, oh, about five-nine and a quarter?

The world's strangest refund? That came from writer James Jones, who had a best seller with his novel, *From Here to Eternity.* Whenever he ran into friends who had read the book, Jones would hand them envelopes containing sixty-seven cents, his royalty share for each book sold.

"I don't want to make money on my friends," he explained.

Can you make a lot of money selling ring tones for cell phones? Yes, if you have ring tones with special powers and buyers with none.

In Hong Kong you can buy ring tones designed to help you lose weight or increase the size of your bust every time someone phones you.

The British doctor Joseph Lister came to the aid of a wealthy man who had a fish bone caught in his throat. After Lister successfully removed the bone, the man asked how he could reward him.

"Suppose," the doctor offered, "we settle for half of what you would be willing to give me if the bone were still lodged in your throat."

Harry Cohn was the tyrannical head of Columbia Studios back in the old days when the movie studios ran the lives of the stars and everyone else who worked for them.

Cohn once turned down a fortune offered for Columbia. A producer asked the boss why he hadn't sold when the sale would have made him rich.

Cohn shrugged and said, "But then who would invite me to dinner?"

It was hard to top the playwright and Algonquin Round Table wit George S. Kaufman. One day over lunch, a businessman boasted that he was a self-made man who'd built a fortune even though he'd been born without a penny to his name.

"When I was born," Kaufman replied, "I owed $12."

The Holy Roman Emperor Charles V owned Malta but rented the island to the Knights of Saint John for the price of one falcon a year. That religious order stayed in Malta for 268 years, or 268 Maltese falcons.

One of them inspired the great crime novelist Dashiell Hammett to write his classic story about the things that dreams are made of, *The Maltese Falcon*.

> **EXPERTS ESTIMATE THAT 20 PERCENT OF ALL THE GOLD EVER DUG OUT OF MINES RESTS ON THE FLOORS OF THE OCEANS IN SUNKEN SHIPS.**

Most people would enjoy living like the rich—if only for a day. But what a surprise to find that the wealthy want to play poor:

1) In the years before the French revolted, Queen Marie Antoinette ordered a rural village built for the amusement of her friends. She moved poor farm families into the village.

   When the pressures of palace life grew too great, the queen and her companions would spend a week pretending to be peasants in their own village. What fun. They'd wear cheap clothes, eat humble meals, tend to the flock. Well, not really tend to the flock, but pretend to.

2) A couple of centuries later, in the allegedly egalitarian United States, there was a craze among East Coast socialites to throw poverty socials at their estates. The elite guests would arrive wearing charmingly ratty clothes and sit down to a hobo meal eaten from tin cans. Those people knew how to have fun.

3) In an odd variation of the poor rich, seventeenth-century British elite developed a passion for ornamental hermits.

Men were hired to live in caves and hollow trees on the grand estates of the aristocracy. Charles Hamilton of Surrey hired a hermit under these conditions:

1) He must never cut hair, beard, or fingernails.

2) He must remain within the confines of the estate.

3) He must never converse with the servants.

If the ornamental hermit lasted under those conditions for seven years, Hamilton would pay him seven hundred pounds. The man chosen for the job lasted three weeks.

The sixteenth-century French King Francois I tired of the effort of retiring to the palace's smallest room to take care of his personal business. He ordered servants to fashion a portable toilet of royal proportions. Then he appointed royal seat-bearers to carry the toilet around wherever he went.

The idea caught on with other people who had too much money. Catherine de Medici had her portable toilet trimmed with blue and red velvet. When her husband died, Catherine's toilet went into mourning—with a black velvet seat suitable for those somber occasions when nature called.

The notion that some people should be assigned to carry around other people's excrement is abhorrent to freedom-loving Americans, who can be seen walking around parks and beaches carrying bags of their dogs' poop with them. What was once the privilege of kings is now the irony of pets.

The rich not only make the big bucks, they make the small ones too.

1) Movie star Gary Cooper paid for all his minor purchases with checks, because merchants wouldn't cash them but would keep the checks as autographs. The artist Marc Chagall tried the same ploy, paying for everything by check. As long as the amount is small, a famous person's signature is worth more in nostalgia than money.

2) The famous artist Pablo Picasso commissioned a cabinetmaker to build an armoire for his house. Picasso drew a sketch showing the craftsman what he had in mind, and then inquired about the cost of the project.

"It will cost you nothing," the cabinetmaker said, "if you sign the sketch."

What would you do if you won a million dollars in the lottery? Fret about how long the money would last? A million dollars doesn't go as far as it used to, so they tell me.

But if you won $7 million, now you've got enough to indulge your fantasies. That's how much Francine Katzenbogen of Brooklyn won in the state lottery. She took her winnings and bought a mansion to create a lavish lifestyle—for her cats.

Katzenbogen had taken care of twenty stray cats before she struck it rich. The lottery gave her enough to buy a million-dollar mansion in LA, rent a cargo plane, and move all her cats to their own mansion on the West Coast.

When people questioned her sanity for spending a fortune on cats, she pointed out, "If I bought jewelry or an expensive car, nobody would think twice or criticize me."

Katzenbogen died at fifty-one before she could spend the fortune she had lucked into. Ironically, relatives claimed that her early death was provoked by asthma aggravated by allergies—to cats.

"I'M NOT A PARANOID, DERANGED MILLIONAIRE," HOWARD HUGHES INSISTED. "GODDAMN IT, I'M A BILLIONAIRE."

When Imelda Marcos, first lady of the Philippines, was put on trial for embezzlement in 1990, she rankled at the parade of witnesses against her.

"I get so tired of listening to one million dollars here, one million dollars there," she sighed. "It's so petty." Those are words we'd all like to be able to live by.

In 1999 a woman counterfeiter was arrested in Sri Lanka for trying to pass a $1 million dollar bill. The U.S. Mint does not print a $1 million dollar bill. Why would it? How many people would ever need one?

When the woman was challenged at a bank, she showed the teller a certificate of authenticity signed by officials of the International Association of Millionaires, an organization that doesn't exist any more than the $1 million bill does.

Million-dollar counterfeiting seems to appeal to women crooks. A Georgia woman was arrested for fraud in 2004 when she walked into a Wal-Mart, wheeled $1,000 worth of merchandise up to the checkout counter, and handed the cashier a $1 million bill. Wal-Mart is well-stocked, but even they can't make change for a $1 million bill.

The wealthy should have more motivation to save the planet than the rest of us. After all, if they save it, they get to keep it. But even in ecology, the rich are different than you and I.

The heiress Betsy Bloomingdale explained in 1982 how she was doing her part to help the country conserve energy: "I ask my servants not to turn on the self-cleaning oven until after seven in the morning."

Thank God some people realize that only your servants can prevent forest fires. They ask not what their country can do for them, but only what their country can do for their investment counselors.

Movie studio chief Samuel Goldwyn wanted to buy the film rights to a play by George Bernard Shaw but thought he could bargain down the asking price by appealing to the playwright's vanity.

Goldwyn explained that if Shaw sold him the play for a reasonable price, "Millions of people would get a chance to see your play who would otherwise never see it. Think of the contribution to art."

Shaw wasn't moved to lower his price, explaining, "The trouble is, Mr. Goldwyn, you think of nothing but art, and I think of nothing but money."

John Milton's *Paradise Lost* is one of the great poems of English literature. In the seventeenth century, the author sold the rights to the first edition to a London bookshop owner for ten pounds.

When Milton died, his wife sold all remaining rights to *Paradise Lost* for an additional eight pounds.

As president of Princeton University before he became president of the United States, Woodrow Wilson objected to colleges that gave out too many honorary degrees to people who had not earned the degrees academically but might donate money to the college fund.

He told the story of one tycoon who was given three honorary degrees, none of which he merited. "The third was given because he had two," Wilson explained, "the second because he had one, and the first because he had none."

After he became a millionaire, John Jacob Astor found he had many relatives he'd never met before. Astor's standard response, when besieged by someone claiming poverty and family ties, was to give the person $5 and be done with him.

One supplicant, displeased by the meager amount of the donation, protested, "Your son just gave me $10."

"I'm not surprised that he did," Astor said. "He has a rich father."

Before writer Mark Twain became rich and famous, he survived in San Francisco on a reporter's meager salary. One day a friend saw Twain carrying a cigar box down the street and stopped him. "I always see you with a cigar box in your hands," the friend said. "I am worried that you are smoking too much."

"I'm not smoking," Twain reassured him. "I'm just moving again."

There are people who make easy money from an astronomical con game where the victims have a choice: they can either pay for a service or get the exact same result for free. They choose to pay.

There are so many billions of stars in the universe, that many of them don't have names. For a price, astronomical con men will name a star after you or anyone else whose name you want to put in heavenly lights.

What they don't tell you: the International Astronomical Union, which keeps track of the thousands of named stars, doesn't recognize stars named by non-astronomers.

How do you get a star officially named after yourself? Sight a star that hasn't already been discovered and apply to the union. Good luck.

Or you could follow Nike's advice and just do it. This is what the ancient Greeks did, which is why we still have stars with ancient Greek names even though there are no more ancient Greeks.

Name that star anything you want. If the official astronomers don't recognize your star, don't recognize theirs. You can still point to the sky and say, "See that 4,070th star on the left? That one's mine."

To celebrate the Christmas season, George Washington signed a contract with his estate gardener, giving the man an extra $4 "with which he may be drunk four days and four nights." A dollar went a lot further in those days, even if you did have to get drunk on schedule.

"I'm so naive about finances," movie star Brooke Shields said. "Once when my mother mentioned an amount, I realized I didn't understand. She had to explain, 'That's like three Mercedes.' Then I understood."

Who is the richest of them all?

Naturalist John Muir claimed that he was richer than millionaire E. H. Harriman. "I have all the money I want," Muir explained, "and he hasn't."

SEVEN

MILO, PUT DOWN THAT TREE: WEIRD WAYS TO DIE

When Henry Palmerston was eighty-one, his doctor told him he would soon die. Palmerston, a former prime minister of England, dismissed the physician, saying, "Die, my dear doctor? That's the last thing I shall do."

And he was right.

Even though we all must go sometime, there are no rules about how. Dying is the last refuge of creativity. Exits give us one last shot at originality.

A champion wrestler of ancient Greece, Milo of Crotona, was always looking for new tests of strength—until he found the wrong one.

Walking through a forest, Milo passed a tree in which a wedge had been abandoned when a woodsman failed to split the trunk. Believing he was strong enough to split the trunk with his bare hands, Milo reached into the crack formed by the wedge and strained with all his might.

He ripped the tree apart far enough to free the wedge. But when the wedge slipped out, the tree snapped back, trapping Milo's arms in the trunk. The mighty Milo died when night and a pack of wolves came.

I n West Germany a bachelor drowned in his kitchen sink while washing up after dinner. He blacked out, fell forward, and drowned in the dishwater.

Yet another advantage of the married life—you can practice the buddy system while cleaning up.

B oxer Stanley Ketchel was a tough customer. An opponent might knock him down during a match, but Ketchel was notorious for getting off the canvas to win fights.

When news of Ketchel's death spread through boxing circles, a friend suggested, "Start counting to ten. He'll get up at nine."

James Henry Smith was a real Pittsburgh Steelers fan. When he died in 2005, his family wanted to remember him doing what he loved best. In the funeral parlor, he was arranged sitting in his recliner, dressed in black-and-gold Steelers pajamas and robe. Cigarettes and a beer were within reach, a remote control in his hand as the TV played Steelers football highlights.

"It was just like he was at home," his sister said. "He loved football, and nobody did anything until the game was over."

Extraordinary parting shots: Have you ever rehearsed what you'd say if you faced a firing squad? It would be a challenge to match the panache demonstrated by these condemned:

1) Armand Lauzun, a French military leader, was sent to the guillotine in 1793 by the bloodthirsty French Revolutionary Committee. Lauzun spent his last moments in a prison cell dining on oysters and fine wine. When the executioner came for him, Lauzun said, "Allow me to finish, citizen, and have a glass of this wine. In your profession you need courage."

2) Margaretha Geertruida Zelle from Holland became famous as Mata Hari, an exotic dancer whose charms won the hearts, and perhaps the military secrets, of officers from both the German and French armies during World War I.

In 1917 the French government put her on trial as a spy. Convicted of crimes she probably didn't commit, Mata Hari played the romantic foreign agent up to the end. On the day of her execution, she dressed in her best clothes: a silk kimono, slippers tied with silk ribbons, a fur coat, hat, and gloves.

Telling the firing squad, "I am ready," she spurned a blindfold and blew the soldiers a kiss before they shot her. Her dashing style so upset the firing squad that many of them missed their target. But not all.

3) The Irish patriot Robert Erskine Childers was stood up in front of a firing squad during the Irish Civil War. "Take a step or two forward, lads," he called to the riflemen. "It will be easier that way."

4) Sir Thomas More, England's lord chancellor, was beheaded at the order of the king in 1535. Feeling weak as he climbed the steps to the scaffold, More said to his escort, "I pray you, Mr. Lieutenant, see me safe up. And for my coming down, let me shift for myself."

> AS MOVIE STAR JOHN BARRYMORE LAY DYING
> IN 1942, HE REASSURED A FRIEND, "DIE? I
> SHOULD SAY NOT, OLD FELLOW. NO BARRYMORE
> WOULD ALLOW SUCH A CONVENTIONAL
> THING TO HAPPEN TO HIM."

British poet A. Alvarez studied the motivations for suicide in his book, *The Savage God.* "No one is promiscuous in his way of dying," he observed. "A man who has decided to hang himself will never jump in front of a train."

George Eastman became wealthy by inventing the Kodak camera in the 1890s. Although he had a fear of dying, he risked his life to hunt bears and tigers. At the age of seventy-eight, Eastman wrote his friends a note, stating simply, "My work is done. Why wait?" Then he shot himself.

Some ironies would be painful if you had time to appreciate them. Consider the Czechoslovakian woman who discovered that her husband was cheating on her. She grew so despondent that she decided to end it all by jumping out her apartment window.

At that very moment, her wayward husband was coming home from one of his dalliances. She landed on top of him. That stopped his philandering because she killed him, which also ended her thoughts of suicide because she survived.

A German woman wasn't so lucky. She was having trouble with a particularly tough crossword puzzle one night. She nudged her husband awake and asked for help with a clue. He gave her the answer and went back to sleep, as she went back to her puzzle.

Stumped again, she woke him again. After the fourth awakening, he flew into a rage and strangled her. He was acquitted on grounds of temporary insanity.

Religious zealots in the Middle Ages burned heretics at the stake for all kinds of reasons and for none at all. Many people who were of a scientific frame of mind, in those dark ages before science, suffered that fate for advancing views that challenged the establishment.

One of the oddest heresies: the Huguenot Bernard Palisay claimed in 1589 that fossils were the remains of living creatures. For maintaining such a radical belief, he was burned alive.

Perhaps you've seen pictures of those ancient Incan ruins—the stone arenas where a game was played with goals scored by throwing a ball through a ring mounted on a stone wall. Maybe you remember that losers of the game were traditionally executed.

Do you know how the winners were rewarded? You might say that not being executed over a game was reward enough. But there was a bonus: The men watching the contest took off all their clothes and gave them to the winners. Even Michael Jordan didn't get that clause in his contract.

When British playwright Ben Jonson died in 1637, he was buried standing up. Why? At the writer's request, King Charles I of England had granted him a square foot in Westminster Abbey, but no more than that.

Upright was the only way the gravediggers could fit Johnson into the space allotted.

The Greek philosopher Diogenes the Cynic asked his friends to bury him facing down to make a statement that the world was a topsy-turvy place.

In philosophical agreement with Diogenes was British Army Major Peter Labelliere, who died in 1800. He insisted that he be buried vertically, headfirst.

"As the world is turned topsy-turvy," Labelliere explained, "it is fit that I should be right at last."

A bar owner in Nicaragua brewed a batch of sugar-cane rum in large cans that had previously contained insecticide. The barkeep was accused of poisoning eleven customers with the rum. He denied the charge. To prove his innocence and the purity of the rum, he drank a large glass—and dropped dead on the spot.

The toughest criticism is self-criticism. Zeuxis, an ancient Greek painter, stepped back from a finished canvas and saw the flaws in his work. He began laughing at himself, couldn't stop, burst a blood vessel, and laughed himself to death.

Seventeenth-century French symphony conductor Jean-Baptiste Lully accidentally killed himself with his own baton. At that time, conductors used large staffs to lead the orchestra. While conducting a performance for the king, Lully smashed his toe with the staff and died from the infection.

The notorious Texas outlaws of the Great Depression, Bonnie and Clyde, were ambushed and gunned down by the law in Gibsland, Louisiana.

Before that fateful rendezvous, the bank-robbing couple had shot their way out of numerous police traps. So when Bonnie and Clyde were finally cornered, the police took no chances and shot them to pieces.

Locals flocked to the site of their slaying and cut down all the trees searching for souvenir bullets. Frank Hamer, the Texas lawman who set the trap for Bonnie and Clyde, ensured their infamy when he stood over their bullet-riddled bodies and remarked, "Well, they died with their guns in their hands."

I rish writer George Bernard Shaw was being witty when he observed that, "Martyrdom is the only way in which a man can become famous without ability." He said that in the 1930s before the stars of television could have changed his mind.

Dark humor from the comic corner of the morgue:

1) Writer H. L. Mencken: "Men have a much better time of it than women. For one thing, they marry later. For another, they die earlier."

2) Comic Richard Jeni: "It is a sad fact that 50 percent of marriages in this country end in divorce. But hey, the other half end in death. You could be one of the lucky ones."

3) Comic Larry Miller: "It's more dangerous to have a clean-living president with his finger on the button. He thinks he's going right to heaven. You want to feel safe? Give me a guy who fights in bars and cheats on his wife. This is a man who wants to put off Judgment Day as long as possible."

Odd last words from two philosophers:

1) As Henry David Thoreau lay on his deathbed, a friend asked if he had made his peace with the Lord. Thoreau's classy response: "I was not aware that we had quarreled."

2) The dying German philosopher Georg Hegel repined, "Only one man ever understood me, and he didn't understand me."

Writer Edward Abbey offered a wilderness explanation for the madness of poets, a kind of dark stupidity that strikes down the too intellectual.

Abbey wrote, "Our suicidal poets (Plath, Berryman, Lowell, Jarrell, et. al.) spent too much of their lives inside rooms and classrooms when they should have been trudging up mountains, slogging through swamps, rowing down rivers. The indoor life is the next best thing to premature burial."

A Japanese doctor loved his wife. When she died in 1959, he embalmed her body. Unable to say good-bye, he kept her in their bedroom for ten years until the police discovered that the doctor had been covering up his wife's death.

To pay his fine, the doctor sold the house. Which is creepier: If the buyer didn't know what had been going on in that house? Or did know and bought it anyway?

However far the mighty may fall, it's not as far as the distant relatives of the mighty.

Consider one of Emperor Napoleon's descendents, an American named Jerome Napoleon Bonaparte. While his forefather conquered Europe, Jerome walked his wife's dog in Manhattan's Central Park in 1945. He died from head injuries sustained when he tripped on the dog's leash.

In the comic movie *Bill and Ted's Bogus Journey,* actor William Sadler plays the Grim Reaper with a Czechoslovakian accent. Sadler is an American. So why the Czech accent?

"I figured the guy is Death," Sadler explained, "he has to come from somewhere. Death is not from New Jersey. So I decided he came from Czechoslovakia."

What would Sadler do if he meets the real Grim Reaper after making fun of him in a movie? "I'll tell him I was just joking," the actor said. "I hope he has a sense of humor."

Unusual legacies:

1) When the wealthy, sophisticated composer Cole Porter died, he left his pianos to the Julliard School of Music so students could study on the keys of the great. He left all his tuxedos and other stylish fashions to the Salvation Army.

Porter also took care of his relatives for years after his death. The rights to his music generated millions, divided by his family.

2) When Bob Fosse, the multitalented Broadway and movie director, died, he left $378.79 apiece to sixty-six friends so that each of them would "go out and have dinner on me."

His guest list included such celebrities as actors Dustin Hoffman, Melanie Griffith, Jessica Lange and Roy Scheider (who played Fosse in the bio-pic *All That Jazz*), writers Neil Simon and E. L. Doctorow, and comic Buddy Hackett.

3) Another dinner-lover was wealthy magazine publisher Malcolm Forbes, who gave $1,000 apiece to the people who ran his favorite Manhattan eateries, "as a token of gratitude for the joy their skills and genius added to the lives of those who've been lucky and sensible enough to dine at their restaurants."

Forbes's favorites: Mortimer's, the Four Seasons, Chanterelle, Le Cirque, Lutece, Bice, Nippon, Le Grenouille, and Benihana.

THE GRIM REAPER HAS A DARK SENSE OF HUMOR, ACCORDING TO THE POET W. H. AUDEN, WHO WROTE: "HE LISTENS TO YOUR CHEST, SAYS—'YOU'RE BREATHING. THAT'S BAD. BUT DON'T WORRY; WE'LL SOON SEE TO THAT, MY LAD.'"

The Japanese eat little fat in their diet and suffer fewer heart attacks than Americans or the British. The French eat a lot of fat, yet also have fewer heart attacks than the British and Americans.

The Japanese rarely drink red wine, while Italians drink a lot of red wine. Both groups have fewer heart attacks than Americans and British.

Medical conclusion: Eat and drink whatever you want. It's speaking English that kills you.

How many of us have not prayed for a miracle in our lives? "Get me out of this. Make me rich. Let me win." The demands never stop coming.

Yet every moment of our lives already qualifies as a miracle. The odds against any of us being here—as a race and as individuals—are so great that each day you continue to exist can be seen as a miracle in a universe that primarily consists of dead space.

Consider this wisdom from economics professor Ludwig von Mises. When the professor turned eighty-eight, a friend asked him how he felt upon awakening each morning.

"Amazed," von Mises explained.

EIGHT

RUNNING DOWNHILL AND OTHER STRANGE LESSONS THEY WON'T TEACH YOU IN SCHOOL

British writer A. A. Milne taught his young son Christopher why the boy should not hold up his fork while dining.

"Suppose someone suddenly fell through the ceiling," the author of *The House at Pooh Corner* explained. "They might land on your fork, and that would be very painful."

Schools may be good at teaching the obvious. But the twisted lessons of life you have to pick up as you go along and from the strangest places.

In the 1930s the Boston Red Sox traded for Smead Jolley, a good hitter but a lousy fielder. For every run he drove in with his bat, his bad glove was likely to let in one for the other team.

The Boston coaches knew Jolley would have trouble adjusting to the irregular outfield in Fenway Park, particularly the slope in front of the wall. So they spent a lot of time teaching him how to run back on long drives and take the hill in stride.

In one game soon after he joined the Sox, Jolley ran back up the slope for a deep fly. He misjudged the ball and had to dash in as it fell short. The clumsy outfielder tripped over his feet and slammed into the ground as the ball rolled away.

At the end of that painful inning, Jolley complained to his coaches that they'd wasted their time training him to go uphill when "there isn't one of you with the brains to teach me how to come down."

The French orchestra leader Pierre Monteux critiqued a concert conducted by a young André Previn, asking the new conductor whether he thought the orchestra had played well.

"I thought they played very well," Previn said.

"So did I," Monteux agreed. "Next time, don't interfere with them."

The human race tends to get raves from the critics, because the reviewers are critiquing themselves. That's how people end up with plugs like:

"At the top of the food chain."

"Made in God's image."

"Smarter than your average bear."

Not all critics are so easily impressed. Take this left-handed review from the English philosopher Bertrand Russell: "If I were granted omnipotence and millions of years to experiment in, I should not think Man much to boast of as the final result of all my efforts."

When Kurt Vonnegut wrote *Slaughterhouse-Five* about the fire bombing of Dresden during World War II, the novel became a rallying point for activists and college students opposed to the Vietnam War.

But Vonnegut didn't think his book would do much good in changing the minds of the people who were actually running the war.

"It's as likely that an antiwar book will stop war," Vonnegut commented, "as it is that an anti-glacier book will stop glaciers."

Physicist Albert Einstein: "The only reason for time is so that everything doesn't happen at once."

Here's a little cultural misunderstanding that led to an avoidable massacre:

In the 1600s Jesuit missionaries explored the northeast regions of the New World, trying to convert the natives to Christianity. The Jesuits believed that by baptizing Indians, their own place in heaven would be assured. But many of the priests got a quicker trip up than they expected.

The Indians thought the Jesuits' ritual was an attempt to kill them, since they always baptized people who were dying. Communion also made the Indians suspicious. They thought the Jesuits were demons for keeping their god in a box and eating him.

The best solution for dealing with such a deadly enemy was to kill the missionaries before they killed you. And that's why many missionaries trying to spread the good word ended up being slaughtered by people who didn't get the message.

And now for twenty-three odd but quick lessons passed along by brilliant teachers from the School of Life:

1) Writer Oscar Wilde: "When people agree with me I always feel that I must be wrong."

2) Writer Kin Hubbard: "A restaurant waiter always lays your check on the table upside down so you won't choke to death."

3) Psychologist Laurence Peter: "Build a better mousetrap and the government will build a better mousetrap tax."

4) TV newsman Eric Sevareid: "The chief cause of problems is solutions."

5) Cartoonist Charles Schulz: "Don't worry about the world coming to an end today. It's already tomorrow in Australia."

6) Comic Steve Landesberg: "Honesty is the best policy. But insanity is a better defense."

7) New York Yankees manager Casey Stengel: "They say you can't do it, but sometimes that isn't always true."

8) Comic Jackie Vernon: "The meek shall inherit the earth. They won't have the nerve to refuse it."

9) Oil billionaire J. Paul Getty: "The meek shall inherit the earth, but not the mineral rights."

10) Poet T. S. Eliot: "The best way to understand a foreign country is by its smell."

11) Magazine editor Christopher Morley: "No man is lonely while eating spaghetti. It requires too much attention."

12) Poet Robert Brault: "The average pencil is seven inches long, with just a half-inch eraser—in case you thought optimism was dead."

13) Playwright George Bernard Shaw: "The reasonable man adapts himself to the world. The unreasonable one persists in trying to adapt the world to himself. Therefore, all progress depends on the unreasonable man."

14) Writer Henry Miller: "The world is not to be put in order. The world is in order. It is for us to put ourselves in unison with this order."

15) Businessman Franklin Jones: "Bravery is being the only one who knows you're afraid."

16) Statesman Lord Palmerston: "Dirt is not dirt, but only something in the wrong place."

17) Writer Bertolt Brecht: "The man who laughs has not yet heard the news."

18) Movie star Robert Mitchum: "No matter what you do, do your best. If you're going to be a bum, be the best bum there is."

19) Professor William Inge: "It is useless for the sheep to pass resolutions in favor of vegetarianism while the wolf remains of a different opinion."

20) Writer William McFee: "The world belongs to the enthusiast who keeps cool."

21) Comic Groucho Marx: "There is only one way to find out if a man is honest—ask him. If he says yes, you know he's crooked."

22) Architect Edward Stone: "Don't be too worthwhile. Always keep a few character defects handy. People love to talk about your frailties. If you must be noble, keep it to yourself."

23) Writer Louise Beal: "Love thy neighbor as thyself, but choose your neighborhood."

One sign of genius is that they enjoy thinking in circles. Take physicist Albert Einstein, who observed: "The most incomprehensible thing about the world is that it is at all comprehensible."

Einstein understood the paradox of his own thinking. "To punish me for my contempt for authority," he said, "fate made me an authority myself."

Physicist Niels Bohr shared Einstein's predicament. They were working scientists trying to understand the secrets of the universe and only reluctant experts. Bohr pointed out, "An expert is a man who has made all the mistakes which can be made in a very narrow field."

Bohr also noted: "The opposite of a correct statement is a false statement. But the opposite of a profound truth may be another profound truth."

What does it take to be a true gentleman? More than manners. Ungracious people may know their forks and glasses but still make you feel miserable. According to one member of that gentleman's club known as England, it requires divine intervention.

"I can make a lord," King James I of England claimed. "But only God Almighty can make a gentleman."

The next time your mom disapproves of your manners, you'll know whom to blame.

Actor Yves Montand demonstrated why the French get away with things that if said by an American would be followed by a slap and a visit from a divorce attorney.

"A man can have two, maybe three love affairs while he's married," Montand explained. "After that it's cheating."

When Oliver Cromwell got involved in England's politics: chaos. But when he sat down to dinner: uncommon good sense, as evidenced by his prayer of grace.

"Some people have food but no appetite," Cromwell would intone at the table. "Some people have an appetite but no food. I have both. The Lord be praised."

Amen, and pass the potatoes.

"I like to think of my behavior in the '60s as a learning experience," journalist P. J. O'Rourke said. "Then again, I like to think of anything stupid I've done as a learning experience. It makes me feel less stupid."

Three quick lessons about the twisted ways of the law:

1) Lawyer Jeremy Bentham: "Lawyers are the only persons in whom ignorance of the law is not punished."

2) Writer Anatole France: "The law, in its majestic equality, forbids the rich as well as the poor to sleep under bridges, beg in the streets, and steal bread."

3) Writer George Bernard Shaw: "The most anxious man in a prison is the warden."

As for happiness, you'll want to keep in mind what Beatrice Arthur has to say in the movie, *Lovers and Other Strangers*: "Don't look for happiness, Richie. It'll only make you miserable."

J. Frank Dobie grew up on a cattle ranch, not a likely candidate to become a university professor teaching poetry. But that's what he did. In his remarkable book, *Cow People*, Dobie recounts the lives of Texas cowboys from the late 1800s.

Here Dobie reflects on photos of old cowboys who lived a rough life of work, drought, wind, and flood: "Look at the faces of people who belong elementally. They may not be sculptured by thought. They never evidence easy success. They reveal a profound chastening."

In search of God and man:

God finds most people through their families, church, or traditions. But some people go on strange searches for God and report back on what they find:

1) Writer Mark Twain: "Man is a creature made at the end of the week's work when God was tired."

2) Writer Bill Vaughan: "Either heaven or hell will have continuous background music. Which one you think it will be tells a lot about you."

3) Poet W. H. Auden: "May it not be that, just as we have to have faith in him, God has to have faith in us and, considering the history of the human race so far, may it not be that faith is even more difficult for him than it is for us?"

4) Scientist Francis Bacon: "Man prefers to believe what he prefers to be true."

5) Poet Heinrich Heine: "God will forgive me. It is his business."

6) Mathematician Blaise Pascal: "If you gain, you gain all. If you lose, you lose nothing. Wager, then, without hesitation, that he exists."

7) Writer George Bernard Shaw: "We are told that when Jehovah created the world, he saw that it was good. What would he say now?"

8) Poet Carl Sandburg: "A baby is God's opinion that the world should go on."

9) Writer Michel de Montaigne: "Few men dare publish to the world the prayers they make to Almighty God."

10) Writer H. L. Mencken: "It is impossible to imagine the universe run by a wise, just, and omnipotent God. But it is quite easy to imagine it run by a board of gods. If such a board actually exists, it operates precisely like the board of a corporation that is losing money."

11) Writer Oscar Wilde: "I sometimes think that God, in creating man, somewhat overestimated his ability."

12) Writer Nicholas Chamfort: "The only thing that stops God from sending a second flood is that the first one was useless."

NINE

THE TWENTY-FIVE-YEAR-OLD TEENAGER AND OTHER WAYS WE GET IT WRONG

"Statistics show," Colorado State Senator Mary Anne Tebedo declared in 1996, "that teen pregnancy drops off significantly after age twenty-five."

Tip to politicos: You will avoid some embarrassment if you never begin a sentence with the words, "Statistics show."

We're not the first people to look into the future and get it wrong. Much of history is the record of what happened that the experts predicted would never happen.

Naval officer Frank Koch was stationed on the bridge of a battleship during night maneuvers in heavy fog when a lookout reported a steady light dead ahead of them.

"Signal that ship we are on a collision course," the captain ordered. "Advise them to change course twenty degrees."

The return signal: "Advisable for *you* to change course twenty degrees."

The battleship captain got angry at being defied and replied: "I'm a captain. Change course twenty degrees."

The response: "I'm a seaman second-class. You better change course twenty degrees."

Furious, the captain sent a third message: "I'm a battleship. Change course twenty degrees."

Back came the message: "I'm a lighthouse."

Celebrities can't get away from their fans, even for a quiet night at the movies. Miami Dolphins football coach Don Shula found that out when he took his family to catch a movie while vacationing in a small town on the coast of Maine.

As Shula and family entered the theater, everyone rose and cheered. "The power of network television is simply amazing," Shula told his wife. "These people must get every Dolphins game all the way up here, and that ovation shows how strongly they feel about football."

As they sat down, a local in the next row turned around and told Shula, "I don't know who you are, but we're really glad to see you. The manager said if he didn't get four more people tonight, he wasn't going to show the movie."

Columnist Heloise, with her helpful household hints, was probably the only person over the age of twelve who knew five hundred useful things to do with empty egg cartons. Some of her readers worked a little too hard to stay one step ahead of her problem-solving tips. Some of Heloise's favorite challenges:

1) Heloise suggested that readers put a cup of liquid in the turkey to keep it moist while roasting. "The turkey turned out great," a reader reported. "But the plastic cup melted."

2) For cleaning that nasty mess out of the bottom of birdcages, Heloise recommended a vacuum. But she neglected to instruct her readers to remove the bird from the cage first. One reader vacuumed the bird right up, but it was saved when her daughter hit the reverse button.

"We all do stupid things," Heloise said when recounting these tales. "But these people actually admit it."

3) Always looking to pass along useful advice from readers, Heloise received a unique solution for a problem many women face: a husband who doesn't help with household chores.

This particularly inventive reader had her husband cremated

when he died. She put his ashes in an hourglass and used them to time her soft-boiled eggs—the first time her husband had done anything useful in the kitchen.

People who work in radio and TV should know: The mike is always live. Even when you think it's off, don't count on it.

Yet scores of professional announcers, broadcasters, and anchors, who have every reason to know better, don't. They get caught saying something when they thought they were off-air that they would never say on-air, except they just did, and it got broadcast to the world.

One of the classic live-mike goof-ups came from Don Carney, who hosted an until-then popular kids' radio show in the '30s. Thinking he was off the air at the end of the show, Carney said to his producer, "That ought to hold the little bastards for another night."

Millionaire heiress Barbara Hutton, who inherited the Woolworth fortune, had strong views on marriage. In 1941, upon divorcing her husband, Count Kurt Heinrich Haughwitz-Hardenberg-Reventlow, Hutton somberly told the press, "I will never marry again."

She felt so strongly about the sentiment that she declared it again in 1945 after divorcing her second husband, movie star Cary Grant. "You can't go on being a fool forever," she explained.

It took Hutton ten years to get around to dumping Baron

Gottfried von Kramm, husband No. 6. "This is positively my final marriage," Hutton promised.

In 1964 Hutton married No. 7, the Vietnamese Prince Doan Vinh de Champacak, and assured the press that he was "a composite of all my previous husbands' best qualities without any of the bad qualities."

Can't beat that combination. Hutton certainly couldn't for two years, after which she divorced No. 7, too.

Scientist Ernest Rutherford won a Nobel Prize for chemistry. But they don't give prizes for scientific predictions. In 1933 Rutherford made this insightful call:

"The energy produced by the atom is a very poor kind of thing. Anyone who expects a source of power from the transformation of these atoms is talking moonshine."

Moonshine has since been outshone by the lights powered by nuclear energy plants.

NINETEENTH-CENTURY IRISH SCIENTIST LORD KELVIN KNEW HE WAS SEEING THROUGH PHONY SCIENCE WHEN HE PREDICTED, "X-RAYS WILL PROVE TO BE A HOAX."

In 1890 physicist Albert Michelson looked at all the inventions and progress made by science and declared, "The more important fundamental laws and facts of physical science have all been discovered, and these are now so firmly established that the possibility of their ever being supplanted in consequence of new discoveries is remote."

About as remote as Albert Einstein.

To their frustration, school kids learn that the value of pi runs on and on—more decimal places than any but the obsessed or a computer would count. The Kansas State Legislature took a reasonable, if unmathematical, approach: It passed a law that rounded pi off to a value of three.

But the Indiana State Assembly disagreed and passed a bill declaring that pi's legal value was 4.0.

In 1973 two French mathematicians tried to settle the matter by publishing a four-hundred-page book, in which they calculated the value of pi to one million decimal places.

How do these rumors get started? Who falls for them? And do you happen to have any 1902 pennies?

In 1906 a rumor spread through the Carolinas and Virginia that 1902 pennies were valuable, because the U.S. Mint had mixed in gold with the copper by mistake when pressing the coins.

People went on a one-cent rampage, buying up every 1902 penny they could find, with prices going as high as a dime a penny. When the government denied the rumor, the speculative market collapsed. People back then actually believed the government when it denied something.

L et's say you were a bank robber. Being a professional in a risky business, would you rob one bank fifty-three times? Or fifty-three banks one time each? And if you did rob fifty-three banks, would you give the police the address of your hideout?

In 1999 an almost-clever Texas swindler took on the IRS by filing fifty-three tax returns electronically—claiming refunds under the names of fifty-three people who were no longer living.

Those refunds added up to over $100,000 in fraudulent returns, but the swindler made one critical mistake. He asked that all the refunds be electronically transferred to the *same* bank account.

Most crooks planning such an audacious crime would have thought about the traceability of so many returns being directed into the same account. This particular thief should have known better. He used to work for the IRS. Eventually, he did know better—as he sat in prison and reflected upon how everything went wrong.

You can always count on male authorities to come up with wacky reasons why women shouldn't be doing what men want to keep for themselves. Back in 1914, it was thinking.

Hans Friedenthal, a Berlin University professor, warned women that "brain work" would cause them to "become bald, while increasing masculinity and contempt for beauty will induce the growth of hair on the face. In the future, women will be bald and will wear long mustaches and patriarchal beards."

Consider yourselves warned.

The telephone may have been hard to invent, but it was more difficult to convince people to use them.

Inventors who competed to develop the first phones were laughed at, ignored, or arrested for their efforts.

In 1865 engineer Joshua Coopersmith tried to raise money to develop a phone system. He was arrested and charged with fraud. In condemning Coopersmith as a con man, the *Boston Post* editorialized: "Well-informed people know it is impossible to transmit the voice over wires, and that were it possible to do so, the thing would be of no practical value."

Judging by the current cell-phone addiction, the paper may have been right about that last charge.

The path to acceptance was no easier for Alexander Graham Bell, who actually produced the first working phone. Bell showed his plans to his future father-in-law, a prominent Boston lawyer named

Gardiner Hubbard, who urged the foolish man who wanted to marry his daughter to give up the effort. Even if he were successful, Hubbard argued, a telephone was "only a toy."

In 1876 when Bell had a functioning phone to demonstrate, he arranged for the president of the United States, Rutherford B. Hayes, to participate in the demonstration. "That's an amazing invention," Hayes acknowledged. "But who would ever want to use one of them?"

If Hayes sounds like a typically slow-dawning politician, let's not forget that Bell offered to sell the telephone to the most advanced technology company of his era: Western Union.

But the telegraph company turned him down. The company's engineering experts looked at the phone and asked themselves: the phone or the telegraph—which holds the key to the future? The experts went with the telegraph.

"This 'telephone' has too many shortcomings to be seriously considered as a means of communication," a Western Union executive concluded in 1876. "The device is inherently of no value to us." Great call.

Another prosecuted inventor: Lee DeForest, whose work on vacuum tubes made radios possible. When DeForest tried to sell stock in his company to develop a radio broadcasting system, he was charged with fraud in federal court.

DeForest didn't get much support from fellow inventor Thomas Edison, who predicted, "The radio craze will die out in time."

Despite his unparalleled success with inventions, Edison was a major failure in the field of prognostication. Consider a few of Thomas Edison's predictions:

1) In 1910 the inventor declared: "In five years more electricity will be sold for electric vehicles than for light."

2) Edison didn't get movies right either, maintaining in 1913, "The talking motion picture will not supplant the regular silent motion picture."

3) As for one of his own major inventions, the phonograph, Edison thought that it was "not of any commercial value."

Arizona State University honored one of the school's best baseball players, who went on to be a great major leaguer, by retiring Reggie Jackson's uniform number: 44.

Diehard baseball fans remembered that when Jackson played at ASU, he didn't wear No. 44. He wore No. 24. But Jackson had become so famous as No. 44 with the Oakland A's and the New York Yankees, that ASU decided to retire a number he'd never worn.

A fad spread through Europe in the fifteenth century, when wealthy sophisticates bought pricey pewter plates for their dining tables. The plates became the silent killers of the Middle Ages.

Food that was highly acidic leached lead from the pewter plates, killing many upper-class diners with lead poisoning. People noticed that this poisoning happened most frequently when tomato sauce was served.

For the next four hundred years, rich Europeans thought tomatoes were poisonous and refused to eat them.

Movies are often miscast. But the Oscar-winning Western *Unforgiven,* which Clint Eastwood starred in and directed, was so obviously written for Eastwood that it's hard to imagine anyone else playing the lead role.

"If I could make a movie as good as *Unforgiven*, I would die happy," said film director Terry Gilliam, who did make a movie that good, *12 Monkeys,* and so has a happy expiration ahead of him.

"Clint Eastwood sat on that script for ten years until he was old enough to play the part," Gilliam said. "*Unforgiven* was originally written for Dustin Hoffman, which shows why writers should never cast their own films."

When Banana Republic expanded from selling clothes into the publishing business, the boss, Mel Ziegler, said his new *Trips* magazine would be "like a good friend at a dinner party telling a wonderful story."

This is a great idea for a magazine. So it's odd that nobody bought it.

Maybe *Trips* appealed only to readers who didn't have good friends, didn't go to dinner parties, and hated wonderful stories. The magazine folded after a single issue.

We understand the important role of critics: to get it totally wrong so we can all have a good laugh at their predictions later on.

It's even funnier when writers look at the work of other writers and come out sounding exactly like the critics they all despise: completely wrong.

1) British playwright Ben Jonson about William Shakespeare: "Players have often mentioned it as an honor to Shakespeare that in his writing, whatsoever he penned, he never blotted out a line. My answer hath been, 'Would he had blotted a thousand.'"

2) Writer Clifton Fadiman about William Faulkner's novel *Absalom, Absalom!*: "The final blowup of what was once a remarkable, if minor, talent."

3) British novelist Virginia Woolf about Irish novelist James Joyce's *Ulysses*: "It is a misfire. It is brackish. It is pretentious. It is underbred, not only in the obvious sense, but in the literary sense. A first-rate writer, I mean, respects writing too much to be tricky."

4) British writer Thomas Carlyle about writer Charles Lamb: "Charles Lamb I sincerely believe to be in some considerable degree insane. A more pitiful, rickety, gasping, staggering, stammering Tomfool I do not know."

5) Poet T. S. Eliot, as a book editor, rejecting novelist George Orwell's *Animal Farm*: "We doubt whether this is the right point of view from which to criticize the political situation at the present time."

    When *Animal Farm* was eventually published, it became a classic political satire that hasn't lost any of its bite, no matter how the political situation changes.

6) Writer William Styron, as a book editor, rejecting explorer Thor Heyerdahl's *Kon-Tiki*: "This is a long, solemn, tedious Pacific voyage best suited to some kind of drastic abridgement in a journal like the *National Geographic*."

    When *Kon-Tiki* was eventually published, after numerous rejections, the true account of Heyerdahl's amazing adventures became a huge best seller.

It's amazing that Hollywood has any stars left when it turns down future greats like these:

1) A Universal Studios exec rejecting an actor in 1959: "You have a chip on your tooth, your Adam's apple sticks out too far, and you talk too slow." Despite all those deficiencies, Clint Eastwood went on to make a career for himself in pictures.

2) But wait: the same Universal exec rejected another actor in 1959, saying, "You have no talent." Some critics might agree, but not the producers who had so many hits with Burt Reynolds.

3) The director of the Blue Book Modeling Agency took one look

at an applicant in 1944 and advised her, "You'd better learn secretarial work or else get married." Instead, Marilyn Monroe went on to become Hollywood's top star.

4) An MGM exec rejected an actor's screen test in 1928: "Can't act, can't sing, balding. Can dance a little." Yep, that would be Fred Astaire.

5) Studio chief Jack Warner gave up on another actor after his screen test: "What can you do with a guy with ears like that?"

Make him the top matinee idol in America? That's what happened when someone saw something besides big ears in Clark Gable.

6) "Doesn't have the presidential look," a United Artists exec said in 1964, rejecting Ronald Reagan to play a president in *The Best Man*.

7) The ultimate Hollywood turndown? That honor goes to Roy Disney, Walt's brother, who in 1937 recommended a drastic move: "He's passé. Nobody cares about Mickey anymore. There are whole batches of Mickeys we just can't give away. I think we should phase him out."

"Disney fires Mickey Mouse." Would have made a great headline, but the little guy managed to squeak through.

Things must go better over in the music world, where talent recognizes talent, right?

1) German composer Johann Scheibe about Johann Sebastian Bach: "His compositions are deprived of beauty, of harmony, and of clarity of melody."

2) German composer Louis Spohr about Ludwig van Beethoven: "An orgy of vulgar noise."

3) Russian composer Peter Tchaikovsky about Johannes Brahms: "What a giftless bastard! It annoys me that this self-inflated mediocrity is hailed as a genius."

4) German composer Moritz Hauptmann about Richard Wagner: "I do not believe that a single one of Wagner's compositions will live after him."

5) The final cruel cut for the classics comes not from another musician but a patron. "Far too noisy, my dear Mozart," the Emperor Ferdinand of Austria advised after the opening of Mozart's opera, *The Marriage of Figaro*, "far too many notes."

O K, so classical composers are kind of catty. But certainly in the world of rock 'n' roll, talent is easier to identify.

1) Here's *Cashbox*, the trade journal for the pop music industry, proclaiming in 1955: "The big question in the music business today is, how long will it last? It is our guess that it won't."

Then there's *Variety*, the other showbiz trade journal, which was more definitive, saying in the same year, "It will be gone by June."

Both publications were predicting the demise of rock 'n' roll itself.

2) "We don't like their sound," a Decca exec said, turning down a chance to sign a British band in 1962. "Besides, guitar groups are on their way out." That group? The Beatles.

Decca had a little problem with talent back then. When the label fired Buddy Holly, an exec declared he was "the biggest no-talent I ever worked with."

3) Keith Moon of the Who was only being helpful when he advised Jimmy Page to give up on his new band. "You'll sink," Moon predicted, "not like a lead balloon but even faster, like a lead zeppelin."

4) In 1963 a British rock promoter wanted to launch a little English band, the Rolling Stones. He told the band there was only one thing holding them back. "Boys, that singer will have to go," he said, referring to Mick Jagger.

5) And let's not forget the advice the manager of the Grand Ole Opry gave to Elvis Presley in 1954: "You ain't going nowhere, son. You ought to go back to driving a truck."

Wait, in the weird world of sports, talent is talent, right? Maybe not.

1) "You've bought yourself a cripple," New York Giants manager Bill Terry ridiculed the Yankees for signing a rookie with a leg

injury. The damaged rookie turned out to be Hall of Famer Joe DiMaggio.

2) On the Giants, a new outfielder made such an unimpressive debut that the *New York Daily News* declared him sourly "just so-so in center field." Yep, another Hall of Famer, Willie Mays.

3) Casey Stengel managed the Brooklyn Dodgers before he led the Yankees to so many World Series. "Kid, you're too small," Casey told a young shortstop at a Dodger tryout. "You ought to go out and shine shoes."

Phil Rizzuto didn't listen to the Old Professor. Instead, he signed with the Yankees and became the best shortstop in the American League, helping the Yanks and Stengel (once he switched teams) win many of those World Series.

4) Over in the NFL, Baltimore Colts owner Robert Irsay drafted a Stanford quarterback in 1983 and then traded him to the Denver Broncos, saying, "He'll never be any good."

True enough, as the rejected John Elway became not a good quarterback but a great one.

5) Speaking of football, here's Robert Saudek, a visionary exec at ABC, predicting gloom and doom for stadiums across the country once television networks started televising games in 1950:

"We'll have silent football. The players won't be bothered by the roar of the crowd, because the crowds will all be watching at home. There'll be no one at the game except the sponsor, and he'll be behind a glass cage."

When it comes to our leaders, we often wonder: How will we survive the next one? Same way we survived all the other incompetents who rose to the top: pure dumb luck.

Here are three leaders who should have known better but managed to look reality in the face and miss it entirely:

1) King Louis XVI of France kept a diary, even though he found one day to be so much like another. Here's his entry for an ordinary day in 1789 — July 14: "Nothing."

   Something must have happened on that day, Louis. What was it? Oh yes, the peasants stormed the Bastille, which led to the French Revolution and a day even the king remembered — his last, spent at the guillotine.

2) Speaking of the French, when the leaders of that country wanted to evaluate the possible combat use of that new invention, the airplane, in 1911, they turned to their leading expert in all things military, Marshal Ferdinand Foch.

   Forget the airplane, Foch recommended. Not for the French. "Airplanes are interesting toys," the war leader explained, "but have no military value."

3) Here's Frank Knox on December 5, 1941: "No matter what happens, the U.S. Navy is not going to be caught napping."

   That was two days before the Japanese attacked and devastated the U.S. Navy at Pearl Harbor. Who was Frank Knox? Secretary of the navy.

TEN

THE EGG WRITER AND THE RELUCTANT ROWER: PEOPLE WHO MAMBO TO THE BEAT OF A DIFFERENT DRUMMER

The eighteenth-century visionary Charles Fourier planned a society in which everyone would eat seven meals a day, five of them salads.

Fourier also believed that sex distracted people too much of the time. So he devised a utopian system where everyone got together one week of the year for unbridled sexual activity. For the other fifty-one weeks: celibacy and salads.

Many stalwart individuals like Fourier march to the beat of a different drummer, although many of them don't need a drummer, and their march may be a mambo.

Henry Pearce, a champion Australian rower, was leading the single scull race in the 1928 Olympics when a mother duck started across the stream followed by her ducklings, paddling directly into the path of his boat.

Pearce pulled in his oars and stopped rowing until the ducks were safely across the water. Then he returned to the race and won the gold.

Pianist and witty writer Oscar Levant was a mass of neuroses, most of which he shared with audiences as comic fodder on radio and TV shows.

When Levant took his army physical for World War II, a draft board official asked him, "Do you think you can kill?"

Reflecting upon his various nervous conditions, Levant replied, "I don't know about strangers—but friends, yes."

William Melbourne, a nineteenth-century British prime minister, found an enthusiastic upside to the death of famous writers. "I am always glad when one of those fellows dies, for then I know I have the whole of him on my shelf," he explained, with the logic of a book collector.

Writers who left behind unfinished manuscripts, to be discovered and published after their deaths, must have driven Melbourne batty.

Melbourne and Margaret Thompson were the kind of wealthy British eccentrics who made England the Home of the Oddballs in the eighteenth century. Mrs. Thompson was a snuff-obsessed tobacco fancier.

When she died in 1776, Margaret Thompson's family followed her explicit instructions for burial. Mrs. Thompson's coffin was stuffed with snuff. Six of her favorite snuff-dippers carried her coffin in the funeral ceremony. They were dressed in snuff-colored clothes. Six young women marched in front of the coffin, passing out snuff to the crowd and scattering snuff to the wind. The minister who performed the service was paid in . . . snuff. This was grand funeral planning not to be sneezed at.

Also English and equally determined to have things his way in all things final: an Englishman named Samuel Baldwin gave instructions for his funeral in 1736. He wanted his body thrown into the ocean. Because he was a sailor? No, so his wife couldn't dance on his grave, which she had often said she would as soon as she could.

The boxer Harry Greb lost an eye fighting in World War I. After the war, he returned to the United States and the boxing ring. Fighting with a glass eye, he turned a handicap into an offensive strategy.

If he was losing, Greb would pop the glass eye out in the middle of a round. If the sight of an eyeball rolling around the ring stunned his opponent, Greb would jump in and knock two-eyes out.

Oddball tacticians like Greb are what referees have in mind when they warn boxers to protect themselves at all times.

Harry Greb wasn't the first fighter to adopt a distraction-by-gross-out offensive strategy. Consider what warriors can learn from that terror of the oceans, the sea cucumber.

When attacked, a sea cucumber vomits. Its vomit is poisonous. Must be a wretched field of study.

Other notable fighters who achieved surprising success with unorthodox combat tactics:

1) His ragtag army was surrounded, low on ammo, and about to be wiped out. How did they rally and win the battle? They called on the sheep, of course, with an assist from the ducks and pigs.

   It happened in 1814 at the Battle of Rancagua, when the Chilean rebels, led by Bernardo O'Higgins, were surrounded by the Spanish army. Their situation looked hopeless. But O'Higgins, who was seriously wounded, had a brainstorm.

   He had his men gather all the animals left in the village: a lot of sheep, a few burros, cows, pigs, dogs, ducks, and chickens. Then they stampeded the animals at the Spanish lines.

Taken by surprise, the Spanish troops spooked and ran. O'Higgins and his men escaped and lived to fight many other days. After four years of revolution, they liberated Chile from the Spanish, and O'Higgins became the new country's first president.

2) During a nineteenth-century naval battle between a ship from Uruguay and one from Brazil, the Uruguayan forces ran out of cannonballs. The resourceful captain loaded the ship's cannons with large wheels of hard cheeses, fired them at the enemy, and took out the mast on the Brazilian ship.

The Brazilian captain realized that withdrawing from the battle was a better tactic than risking defeat at the hands of the original cheese heads.

3) A male camel gets the upper hand by spitting in the rival camel's eyes.

Samuel Ferdinand-Lop ran for the presidency of France in the 1940s on a promise to improve the air quality in Paris by moving the city to the country. Despite his rare common sense, he never got elected.

Lop even wrote his own campaign song. Borrowing the tune from *The Stars and Stripes Forever*, he changed the lyrics to: "Lop, Lop, Lop Lop Lop, Lop Lop Lop! Lop Lop Lop, Lop Lop Lop, Lop Lop Lop Lop!"

Samuel Ferdinand-Lop understood the importance of name recognition among voters.

Most people do the same old job the same old way. Then there are workers who will never fit into the cubicle mentality.

1) The French writer Marcel Proust spent fifteen years writing a sixteen-book novel, *Remembrance of Things Past*. Even for a writer, Proust had unusual work habits. He wrote most of the endless epic lying in bed covered with blankets and scarves, even during the hot, humid Parisian summers.

   He had his windows sealed shut and the walls of his writing room lined with cork to block out street noise.

2) Which great composers wrote music while reclining, not in bed, but in the bathtub? That would be Beethoven and Franz Schubert. Not in the same tub, though.

3) When a minister starts his own church, he may have trouble drawing a congregation. In nineteenth-century England, the Rev. "Mad Jack" Alington had no trouble attracting worshippers. He gave his congregation free brandy and preached free love. He took to the pulpit dressed in leopard skins and delivered his sermon while riding his wooden hobbyhorse.

4) Novelist Harold Robbins wrote in a studio in France, located on the roof of his Mediterranean villa. To get into the studio, he had

to climb a ladder. When he wanted to write, he pulled the ladder up after him so no one could interrupt him.

P eople in creative professions find their inspiration anywhere they can:

1) The wife of writer Robert Louis Stevenson was awakened one night by her husband's agonized cries as he slept. Realizing he was having a disturbing nightmare, she roused him.

"Why did you awaken me?" Stevenson scolded her. "I was dreaming a fine bogey tale."

Stevenson remembered enough of the nightmare to turn it into one of his most famous stories, *The Strange Case of Dr. Jekyll and Mr. Hyde.*

2) Songwriter Paul Simon stumbled onto the unusual title for his song "Mother and Child Reunion." He was inspired by a chicken-and-egg dish with that name on a menu in a Chinese restaurant.

3) German composer Robert Schumann said that his music was dictated to him by angels. Schumann later suffered from hallucinations and spent the last two years of his life in a mental institution.

4) In 1999 a New York performance artist put on an exhibit of the merchandise she had shoplifted, accompanied by a videotape of herself shoplifting. One woman's crime is the same woman's art.

Sometimes reverse inspiration is the best motivator:

1) Elvis Presley had a unique motivation to become the king of rock 'n' roll. "I wanted to be a singer," he said, "because I didn't want to sweat."

2) Movie star Lee Marvin said he learned to act in the Marines, trying to act unafraid during combat. He won a Purple Heart in World War II during the bloody invasion of Saipan.

3) "I wasn't driven to acting by an inner compulsion," movie star Paul Newman admitted. "I was running away from the sporting goods business."

Nancy Luce was both a poet and egg farmer from that island of artists and other eccentrics, Martha's Vineyard, off the coast of Massachusetts. Her eccentricity wasn't the way she wrote poetry but the way she wrote eggs.

On every egg she sold, Luce wrote the name of the bird that had laid it. She was the rare farmer who gave credit to those who did the hard labor, although most hens prefer to work in anonymity, like most poets.

Even among eccentric English noblemen, Matthew Robinson was an eighteenth-century standout. Robinson spent most of the daylight hours soaking in a large outdoor bathtub on his estate. Meals were served in his tub. Visitors were received tub-side, where they were surprised to see the lord surrounded by floating roasts and bobbing potatoes.

The visionary Charles Cros petitioned the French government for funds to build the world's largest magnifying glass. Cros intended to aim the glass at the surface of Mars and etch a greeting into the ground — a *bon jour* from the French to the Martians.

Governments throw away millions of dollars on seemingly sensible ideas that turn out to be a total waste of time and money. But come up with a monumental idea of absurd proportions and suddenly they're all fiscally responsible.

After the Russian Revolution, a Soviet orchestra called the Pervyi Simfonicheskyi Ensemble demonstrated their socialist spirit by eliminating the imperialist position of conductor. To the surprise of music lovers and musicians, the orchestra performed very well without a conductor, giving concerts around the world.

But after four years of egalitarian music, some orchestra members led a revolt, accusing the first violinist of usurping authority by trying to keep time for everyone. Squabbling led to factions, and the orchestra disbanded.

"I'm an alcoholic. I'm a drug addict. I'm homosexual. I'm a genius," writer Truman Capote said in a fit of self-revelation. "Of course, I could be all four of those dubious things and still be a saint."

When he was a lawyer, years before becoming president of the United States, Calvin Coolidge dropped into a tavern that offered a special: two martinis for twenty-five cents.

Coolidge drank one, then headed for the door, telling the bartender, "I'll be back tomorrow for the other one."

If you were rich and had no one around to tell you not to bother, you might decide to straighten out the world. That's what wealthy author Anne Rice tried to do in 1996 when she bought a two-page ad in the *Hollywood Reporter*, the movie industry's trade journal.

Rice, who wrote *Interview with the Vampire*, called the ad: "A Personal Letter to President Clinton," under the belief, apparently, that the president had his mail delivered by the *Hollywood Reporter*.

"Do away with the immensely expensive and demoralizing IRS and the welfare system," Rice advised the president.

"We are rich enough as a nation to share a flat minimum income with those who register for it, leaving them free to work as much as they can and will."

Once she had solved the problems of taxes and unemployment,

Rice quickly moved on: "Let's give America faith again in its government. Let's stop paying people to stay poor, stay disabled, and/or dishonest. Decriminalize drugs. Try to get medical care for all.

"Can't you put it to a national 1-800 number vote?" Rice asked. "Let the people speak."

President Clinton didn't listen to Anne Rice, or to anyone else by his second term. Judging by how much things have improved in the last decade, no one else listened to Rice either. Except, perhaps, for Rice's vampires, who don't pay taxes, go on welfare, work, or require medical care.

For a free-spirited comedian, there's something oddly repressed about Robin Williams. You see it in his movies, where he has played a lot of trapped characters.

In *Jumanji*, Williams spent twenty-six years trapped inside a magical board game. He was the genie trapped in a bottle in *Aladdin*, the boy trapped in the body of a middle-aged Peter Pan in *Hook*, and a man trapped in a woman's clothes in *Mrs. Doubtfire*.

Considering all the personalities Williams has released upon the world through his comedy, what exactly could he have left inside to repress?

Archaeologists have popped one-thousand-year-old popcorn. Why archaeologists can't get anything fresher is not clear.

Mystery writer Agatha Christie offered a clue to the mystery of ancient appeal when she married an archaeologist and declared, "An archaeologist is the best husband a woman can have. The older she gets the more interested he is in her."

W hy you never want to invite an actor to your wedding: When writer and actress Cornelia Otis Skinner was preparing to get married, she asked her father to give her away at the ceremony.

At the wedding rehearsal, the minister explained to her father, the larger-than-life stage actor Otis Skinner, that he would ask him, "Who gives this woman?"

Otis wanted to know what his line would be in response. "You don't answer anything," the minister explained. "You simply hand her over."

"Nonsense," Otis declared. "I've never played a walk-on in my life."

R obert Traub's overriding passion was not his work as a medical microbiologist, but his lifelong study of the flea. His private collection of 2,200 species of fleas was topped only (no, not by your dog) by London's Natural History Museum.

To most people, Traub's work may seem obscure, pointless, and itchy. His research didn't even lead to a better flea collar. But by studying the evolution of fleas and their host animals, Traub rewrote the theory of continental drift and turned around the field of historic geography.

ELEVEN

THE EMPEROR'S BARBER AND OTHER ODD JOBS

I once had an editing job on a magazine where I would cross out parts of well-written articles, then rewrite in pencil the same words I had just crossed out.

This demonstrated to the publisher that I was making major efforts to improve the magazine. He never looked at the actual writing or the quality of the editing, only at the quantity of the editing marks on the manuscript pages.

I'm not the only one with a passion for odd jobs and for the absurdity of spending our lives doing something we wouldn't do if we could figure a way around it.

"I have long been of the opinion that if work were such a splendid thing," the British politician Bruce Grocott said, "the rich would have kept more of it for themselves."

Since few of us can avoid work, let's take a break and look at how nutty the jobs can be.

When the Holy Roman Emperor Joseph II was traveling through France in 1781, he rode ahead of his guards and ministers. Wishing to enjoy a brief anonymity, he took a room at an inn.

The innkeeper, anticipating the arrival of the emperor and his party, asked the stranger if he was in the emperor's employment.

"Yes," Joseph replied, "I shave him sometimes."

And now for something completely different: physicist Wolfgang Pauli.

When he hired a lab assistant, Pauli described the work this way: "Your job is, every time I say something, contradict me with the strongest arguments."

Zalman Bernstein, a Wall Street broker in the 1970s, was a tough boss who conducted unique job interviews. Applicants had to play chess or backgammon against Bernstein so he could get a sense of their intelligence, guile, and nerve.

Like a prototype for Donald Trump, Bernstein would blow cigar smoke in the applicants' faces while they played to test how they performed under duress.

When writer Douglas McGrath graduated from Princeton in 1980, he didn't know what to do next. So he did nothing.

"I don't recommend it as a job strategy," he said. McGrath got lucky. He landed a job as a writer on TV's *Saturday Night Live*.

"All the old stars had just quit," he recalled. "So had the writers. They were desperate for material. I could only have been hired at such a time.

"Doing *SNL* is like being inside a washing machine for a year. Each week the show comes at you like a freight train. The actors do a dress rehearsal right before the show goes on the air. So at 10 p.m. they will tell you to cut two minutes from your sketch."

McGrath considered his main accomplishment on *SNL* to be surviving until he could make movies instead. "I helped inaugurate the era when it became not so smart to hurry back from that party to see the show," he recalled.

The Great Rule of Business: the more absurd the job, the higher up the person who wants it done.

Catherine the Great, empress of Russia, employed a servant whose job it was to tickle the royal feet. Can't you see every brown nose in Russia lining up with their feathers to apply for that position?

The empress wasn't the first elitist tickler-employer. One of the wealthiest men in ancient Rome, Lucullus, threw elaborate dinner parties, complete with tickle slaves. Their job was to tickle his guests' throats with feathers so they would vomit up one huge meal in order to have room to consume another.

The work week has changed over the decades from work-till-you-drop to fourteen hours a day, twelve hours, ten, and now, generally, eight hours a shift.

No matter how much you work, one aspect of the job remains the same, as writer William Faulkner pointed out:

"One of the saddest things is that the only thing that a man can do for eight hours a day, day after day, is work. You can't eat eight hours a day, nor drink for eight hours a day, nor make love for eight hours. All you can do for eight hours is work. Which is the reason why man makes himself and everybody else so miserable and unhappy."

In Victorian London, Mary Ann Smith provided working men with the city's strangest wake-up service. She walked the working-class neighborhood early each morning with her peashooter, waking her clients by peppering their windows with peas.

What happens when the boss sets the benefits for the boss? You get the town council of Mulazzo, Italy.

In 2004, council members voted to reimburse themselves for cosmetic surgery because their appearances were of governmental importance "in the context of the interpersonal and inter-institutional relationships that the governing majority must undertake in providing synergetic assistance toward the pursuit of the objectives established in the platform."

Also, they got tired of looking at each other's ugly faces at council meetings.

If you hire smart people, give them a quiet place to work. But if intelligence isn't a job qualification, then turn up the music.

Studies show that people of higher intelligence have more trouble performing tasks when working in a noisy place, while people of lower intelligence work better when it's noisy.

That should start some good, loud arguments around the copy machine.

I f you're the assistant commissioner for business development in the Texas Department of Agriculture, your main job is to promote Texas beef. That's why it was surprising when Diane Smith, who held that office in 2002, admitted that she had been a vegetarian for fourteen years.

O ne night Leopold Stokowski was conducting the Philadelphia Orchestra in a performance of Beethoven's *Leonora* Overture No. 3, which calls for a trumpet to be played offstage from the wings.

Stokowski was outraged when only silence came from the offstage trumpet. The conductor raced into the wings, where a stagehand had grabbed the trumpet away from the musician. "You can't blow that damn thing here, I tell you," the stagehand said. "There's a concert going on."

R esearchers find that workers are breaking into crying fits on the job more frequently than they used to. Show that research to your boss. If it makes him laugh, then you have the kind of boss likely to increase the national on-the-job tear rate.

It will probably not be a major surprise that studies show women cry four times as frequently as men. Of course, they have men to cry about.

When the prolonged Civil War caused a labor shortage in the federal government, Francis Spinner, who ran the U.S. Treasury, shocked the nation by hiring women clerks for what had previously been an all-male department.

Spinner declared the experiment a great success. Not only did the women do a superior job than the men they replaced, but they did it for half the pay.

Big business followed the government lead by hiring women workers only when it suited an administrative purpose. The first professional telephone operators were sisters — Stella and Emma Nutt — hired by the Boston phone company, because their voices were more soothing and their fingers more nimble than men's. Also, they worked a lot cheaper.

For years, Bert Parks hosted the Miss America Pageant. When the pageant bosses wanted to update the beauty contest's image, they got rid of Bert. What did he do next? Emceed the All-American Glamour Kitty Contest, of course.

Did he sing to the winning cat? You bet. Bert sang, "There she is . . . the Glamour Kitty of America. There she is . . . the kitty queen of the year." Makes you kind of tear up, doesn't it?

In Landes, France, shepherds found that their flocks preferred to slog through the area's watery bogs and marshes. Instead of fencing off the swampy ground to keep out the sheep, the shepherds learned to walk on stilts to keep their shoes and pants dry as they followed their flocks.

"Studio executives are intelligent, brutally overworked men and women who share one thing in common with baseball managers," screenwriter William Goldman said. "They wake up every morning of the world with the knowledge that sooner or later they're going to get fired."

Cynthia Payne appeared to be a normal middle-class housewife, until the English police arrested her for running a brothel in 1987. She beat the charge in court and then described the work of being a madam from a British perspective. "I know it does make people happy," she said. "But to me it is just like having a cup of tea."

Stars may be born, but Oscars are made. The sixty Oscar statues needed for the annual ceremony are manufactured in a day by a Chicago trophy company.

Like the dreams of Tinseltown, they're not solid gold. Oscars are a pewter base electroplated with copper, nickel, a silver flash, and a 24-karat gold finish. But it's thicker than ordinary gold plating.

Do movie stars need a thicker coating because they bounce those Oscars off each other's heads? From time to time. But that's not why they thicken the gold plating.

Many of the stars live in Malibu or other beach colonies on the Southern California coast. The ocean air would corrode the statues if they weren't protected by an extra thickness of gold.

Stars may age, despite the best efforts of their plastic surgeons. But Oscar winners don't have to worry about their statues aging. The manufacturer has a standing offer to replate any Oscar that wears out.

One of the hot non-paying jobs for an outsider with a Hollywood crush is to be chosen as a seat-filler for the annual Oscar TV show. Among the requirements: you must have your own tux or evening gown and like to sit down.

Your job, if you are chosen, is to wait out of sight within the auditorium, ready to sit at a second's notice. When a celebrity goes to the can or outside to grab a smoke, you're rushed in to take that celeb's seat.

Why is that even remotely important? Because the TV cameras keep scanning the audience, and the producers don't want the auditorium to reveal seat gaps.

At the 1995 show, a seat filler (one of my Oscar spies) was sent to fill a chair next to actress Jamie Lee Curtis. But the star turned her away and sent her back. Why? Curtis was unescorted and didn't want to sit next to a woman.

Among the seat-filler rules: no camera, no autographs, stay away from the bar, and don't crash the big party afterward. But, for a few minutes, your butt gets to squiggle down where a famous butt just perched.

Football star Howie Long put it all on the line in the NFL for thirteen rough years. Then he retired and moved on to a second career in television, commercials, and film, starring in a movie called *Firestorm*.

Long saw similarities between working in film and football: "In movies the grips and all the folks on the crew toil in the mud and rain like linemen," Long said.

"By the end of production, you've been through an entire sixteen-game season—except for one difference: When a football season would end for me, I would check myself into the hospital and get my annual operation."

Another difference between the gridiron and a movie set: the way you run. Football is all about quickness. Movies are about fake quickness.

"The running is weird because you have to slow down when you run," Long said. "They want you to do a movie run. You have to give the impression that you're running full speed, but you're not, because the camera can't keep up with you if you did."

Similarly, the fight scenes are exaggerated and slower than real life. "They want you to sell your punches," Long said. "The punch you throw in a movie wouldn't work in real life. They want you to back up to Cleveland and throw it to Des Moines."

The working life of a writer? If you're a successful playwright like Oscar Wilde, it goes like this: "I was working on the proof of one of my poems all morning and took out a comma," Wilde reported. "In the afternoon I put it back again."

> WHEN IS WORK FUN? WHEN YOU'RE VERY, VERY LUCKY. PITTSBURGH PIRATES' SLUGGER WILLIE STARGELL WAS THAT LUCKY. OR AS HE PUT IT, "THE UMPIRES ALWAYS SAY, 'PLAY BALL.' THEY DON'T SAY, 'WORK BALL.'"

Christopher Hart had one of the most unusual specialties in Hollywood. A magician known for his sleight-of-hand work, Hart landed the role of Thing, the disembodied hand in the Addams Family movies.

To audition for the puppet part, Hart competed against other magicians and puppeteers. "I had to show how my hand could display various attitudes," he said. But Hart couldn't use an actor's tools to express emotions. "There are no eyes on the hand," he explained. "You can't tap into the soul of the character that way."

How did Hart's hand handle its newfound fame? "When people find out I'm Thing, they want me to crawl up their arm," he said. "The hand is a celebrity. My hand is working more than I am."

Sometimes the best way to get the job done is by not trying too hard. John Huston was a screenwriter who wanted to direct movies. Howard Hawks, who directed Huston's script for *Sergeant York*, suggested that the studio give Huston a shot at helming a film.

Huston plunged into writing an original screenplay to use for his directorial debut. But the veteran Hawks told him to stop writing. Learning how to direct would be hard enough. Instead, Hawks suggested that Huston make a movie of Dashiell Hammett's mystery novel, *The Maltese Falcon*.

Huston pointed out that *The Maltese Falcon* had already been made into movies twice (under other titles), and both films had flopped.

Hawks explained the problem with the first two versions: their directors had rewritten Hammett's book. "He's one of the best writers in his field," Hawks said. "You do it the way he wrote it."

Huston did just that, creating a film classic by closely following the book (a practice alien to Hollywood). By not doing too much, Huston became one of Hollywood's hottest directors.

B everly Hills Police Detective Paul Edholm Jr. worked for Holly-wood as a garbologist, showing movie directors how a police expert finds evidence in the trash.

But Edholm doesn't think much of the way movies and TV shows capture the working life of cops.

"Ninety percent of police work is so boring, it's ridiculous," he said. "The other 10 percent is pure terror. No one would go see movies about what it's really like."

TWELVE

INTO THE HAREM AND
OTHER TWISTED SURPRISES

Frederick North, an eighteenth-century British statesman, was visiting an Algerian ruler and asked if he might be given a tour of the dey's harem.

The dey looked the Englishman over and said, "He is so ugly, let him see them all."

You've probably had your share of pleasant surprises and your fill of rude awakenings—although not often, like North, at the same time.

During the 2004 baseball season, Best Catch of the Year should have gone to a Cincinnati Reds fan who caught the fortieth homer hit by Reds slugger Adam Dunn.

A TV station interviewed the man, and college police at Miami (Ohio) University didn't drop the ball either. They recognized the fan and served him with an outstanding arrest warrant.

> IN CHINA, TWO HUNDRED RESTAURANTS WERE CLOSED IN 2004 BY GOVERNMENT OFFICIALS, WHO DISCOVERED THE COOKS WERE ADDING OPIUM TO THE FOOD.

When he was a young TV reporter, British actor Richard Whiteley interviewed a farmer in the uplands of Wensleydale. When they were done, Whiteley asked the farmer if he knew the time. He was surprised to see the old farmer crouch down beside a cow, lift the cow's udder, and say, "Ten to one."

"We were amazed," Whiteley recalled. "How can you tell the time by feeling a cow's udder?" he asked.

The farmer offered to show him. "If you crouch down like this," he demonstrated, "and lift up the udder, you can just see the church clock across the valley."

As chaplain of the U.S. Senate, the Rev. Edward Everett Hale was asked if he prayed for the senators.

"No," he said, "I look at the senators and pray for the country."

When is it better to lose than win? When you're playing for the Pittsburgh Pirates. In the first World Series ever played, the Boston Americans beat the Pirates five games to three (it was a best-of-nine Series back then). The Pirates' owner rewarded the Pittsburgh team for a great season by throwing his share of the gate receipts into the pot to be divided among the players.

That's how each player on the losing team walked away with more money than the winners. Sometimes it pays to lose.

TV and movie star Adam Sandler found himself in a familiar situation for those with famous faces. He was on vacation with his family in New Hampshire when they stopped for pizza.

"Hey, you look like Adam Sandler," the kid behind the counter said. "What's your name?"

"Adam Sandler," the star admitted.

"Whoa," the kid said, "that's a coincidence."

When Italy became a nation in 1861 (united from different cultures and city states), only 3 percent of the new country's people could speak Italian.

> THERE ARE BUTTERFLIES IN BORNEO
> LARGER THAN OWLS. NOT BIG OWLS,
> BUT STILL LARGER.

Cleanliness wasn't always next to godliness. In some places it was illegal.

When the bathtub was invented in 1842, it was considered an outrage. In proper Philadelphia, taking a bath was illegal from November through March. In Boston taking a bath was legal, but only if you had a doctor's prescription.

If you look closely, you'll see that different clocks throughout the movie *Pulp Fiction* have the same time: 4:20.

In the movie *Fast Times at Ridgemont High*, the score of the big football game is posted on-screen as 42-0.

What's the favorite date and time for Grateful Dead fans to get married? April 20 (4/20) at 4:20 in the afternoon.

Is there something tricky going on? Yep—420 is code for "likes to smoke pot." Why? Lots of theories about how that got started:

Theory 1) A group of high school students in Northern California used to get together after school at 4:20 to get high. That became shorthand for telling friends what you were doing that afternoon.

Theory 2) The unofficial National Smoke-in Day for pot smokers is 4/20, to console themselves after the downer of tax day on 4/15.

Theory 3) In some cities, 420 is police code for busting people who smoke grass.

Theory 4) There are 420 chemicals in marijuana; and THC, the one that gets you high, is the 420th.

Theory 5) The narcs have 419 better things to do than bust people for smoking pot, so naturally they do the 420th.

Do you suffer from headaches or insomnia? Do you keep a diary? Psychology researchers claim there's a correlation.

On the bright side, people who can't sleep at night have more time to write in their journals.

Do men and women really want different things? Sure. For example, they want each other. What could be more different than that?

Take a look at the adjectives women use most frequently to talk about themselves in personal ads: sensitive, easygoing, attractive, and curvaceous—even though men, in their personal ads, say they want women who are outgoing and athletic.

As for men, they're most likely to describe themselves as honest, caring, humorous, and a financial success—which is precisely what women in their personal ads write that they want in a man.

When Abraham Lincoln was president, a friend came to visit at the White House and was surprised to find the nation's leader polishing his boots instead of leaving the job to a servant.

"You're the president," the friend pointed out. "Why are you polishing your own boots?"

Lincoln shrugged and asked, "Whose boots should I be polishing?"

The writer Joseph Conrad received a letter from the English government, its envelope marked: "On His Majesty's Service." Assuming it contained a demand for back taxes, Conrad simply didn't open the envelope.

After several weeks, an official from the prime minister's office called upon Conrad to find out why the writer had not responded. That's when Conrad learned that the dreaded envelope contained an offer of British knighthood.

One perk of being a Hollywood big shot: you get invited to free movie screenings before the films open in theaters. Or is that one of the drawbacks?

Terry Gilliam, who directed *12 Monkeys*, found himself movied-out in 1967. "I was living with an English girl in LA," the director recalled. "She was a journalist, so we could go to screenings every day of the week. And after about a month of this, I realized I *hated* movies and stopped going."

He may have stopped watching movies, but he kept making them: *Monty Python and the Holy Grail, Time Bandits, The Meaning of Life, Brazil, The Fisher King,* and *The Adventures of Baron Munchausen,* among others.

Ancient Egyptians used a preservative powder called asphaltum to embalm mummies. Centuries later, tomb raiders reversed the process, powderizing mummies so the asphaltum could be mixed into paints.

Some of the old masters you see on your next trip to the museum may have been painted with mummy paint—a strange kind of afterlife.

An exuberant fan of Irish writer James Joyce asked the author, "May I kiss the hand that wrote *Ulysses*?"

Joyce refused the request, explaining, "It did lots of other things too."

> IN 2002 A BRITISH WOMAN TRYING TO
> RAISE MONEY FOR A CHARITY TOOK A BATH
> IN A TUB FILLED WITH TEN GALLONS OF
> MAGGOTS. SHE STAYED IN THE TUB
> FOR ONE AND A HALF HOURS.

In old England, if a husband was dissatisfied with his wife or needed some extra cash, he could sell her. First record of a husband selling his wife comes from 1533. Scholars have turned up documentation for hundreds of wife transactions thereafter. In 1800 a man from Stafford, England, took his wife to the local marketplace and put her up for auction. The bidding began at one penny. He eventually sold her for five shillings and six pence.

This practice was so ingrained in English life, that England abolished slavery before it abolished wife-selling in the late nineteenth century.

As writer Germaine Greer said, "Women have very little idea of how much men hate them."

Bennett Cerf, the publisher who ran Random House during its glory years, had under contract many great writers, including William Faulkner, Eugene O'Neill and John O'Hara. But, Cerf used to tell people, only one of his writers was a genius — and that was Dr. Seuss.

New York Yankee manager Casey Stengel approached one of his players, Bob Cerv, in the dugout after a game, struggling with a baseball manager's toughest responsibility. Then he figured out how to handle it. "Nobody knows this," Stengel whispered to Cerv, "but one of us has just been traded to Kansas City."

Happy-happy are the guiding words of Hollywood movies. Everything works out happily in the vast majority of films.

In the comedy *Three Men and a Little Lady*, actress Fiona Shaw was figuring out how to play a scene where she had just lost the leading man. "I told the director that I should be sad, because I had lost Tom Selleck in the end," Shaw recalled. "So the director said, 'All right, be sad, but in a happy way.'"

Critic Robert Benchley complimented writer John O'Hara on his new play, *Pal Joey*. "I just saw the play again," Benchley enthused, "and I liked it even better than the first time."

O'Hara, touchy like many writers, demanded, "What was wrong with it the first time?"

British actors Robert Morley and Llewellyn Rees ran into each other after a long absence. "It's nice meeting old friends," Rees said. "A lot of people think I'm dead."

"Not if they look closely," Morley commented.

Henry Palmerston, an English prime minister in the 1800s, was proud of his country. A flattering French statesman remarked, "If I were not a Frenchman, I should wish to be an Englishman."

"If I were not an Englishman," Palmerston riposted, "I should wish to be an Englishman."

Otto Kahn was a wealthy American businessman of the 1920s. He was displeased when the owner of a cheap store tried to take advantage of his name by posting a sign in his window: "Abram Cahn, cousin of Otto Kahn."

The millionaire's lawyers threatened to sue the shopkeeper if the sign was not immediately removed and the outrageous claim quit.

The next time Otto drove past the store, he saw a different sign in the window: "Abram Cahn, formerly cousin of Otto Kahn."

Winning isn't everything in baseball. There's also getting the wacky quote just right after the game:

1) Baltimore Orioles pitcher Jim Palmer was feuding with Boston Red Sox manager Darrell Johnson. Palmer claimed he had been misquoted in a newspaper story. "I did not call Johnson an idiot," Palmer argued. "Someone else did. I just agreed."

2) Outfielder Alex Johnson wasn't a slugger. A sportswriter noted that in 1971 Johnson hit only two home runs for the California Angels, but the next year he upped his total to eight homers when he played for the Cleveland Indians. "What's the difference?" the writer asked.

   "Six," Johnson explained.

3) As the Brooklyn Dodgers got ready to play the 1952 World Series against the heavily favored New York Yankees, an angry Dodger manager Charlie Dressen confronted one of his pitchers, Billy Loes, about hurting team morale. "The paper says you picked the Yankees to beat us in seven games," Dressen said. "What's wrong with you?"

   "I was misquoted," Loes explained. "I picked them to win in six."

At a dinner party, an aging Senator Chauncey Depew was sitting next to a young woman who wore a revealing, low-cut dress. He leaned over and asked, "My dear, what is keeping that dress on you?"

"Only your age, Senator," she replied.

English playwright James Barrie invited a friend and his family to join him in his theater box for a performance of *Peter Pan*. After the play ended, Barrie asked the friend's little boy which part of the play he had liked the most.

"What I liked best," the boy said, "was tearing up the program and dropping the bits on people's heads."

When William Jennings Bryan ran for the presidency in 1900, he was so confident of victory that he told a rally: "Friends, tonight my little wife will be going to sleep in a cramped hotel room on the other side of town. But come next March, she'll be sleeping in the White House."

As the cheers from Bryan's supporters died down, a man who favored the opposition candidate, William McKinley, shouted, "If she does, she'll be sleeping with McKinley, because he's going to win."

When quarterback Steve Spurrier played for the Tampa Bay Buccaneers in 1976, the team lost every game that year. In the middle of their terrible season, Coach John McKay tried to rally the players by "emphasizing that games are lost in the trenches by failing to block and tackle on the front lines," Spurrier remembered.

"As the coach is talking, he notices a lineman asleep in the back of the room. McKay wakes him up and asks, 'Where are most games lost?'

"And the lineman says, 'Right here in Tampa, sir.'"

Charlie Finley, the cantankerous owner of the Kansas City Athletics, announced he was moving the team west to Oakland in 1967. Missouri Senator Stuart Symington was sorry to see the team go, but not Finley, a difficult owner who often offended fans, players, and anyone else in his way.

"The loss of the A's," Symington announced, "is more than recompensed by the pleasure of getting rid of Mr. Finley. Oakland is the luckiest city since Hiroshima."

Kansas City later was happy to get the Royals as their new team, but Finley's contentious A's won Oakland four world championships.

Back in Hollywood's golden era, movie studios hired famous novelists and playwrights for the prestige of having them on staff. One movie exec telegrammed America's premier playwright,

Eugene O'Neill, and asked him to come out to Hollywood and work on a script.

The exec requested that O'Neill wire back his response in twenty words or less. Here it is: No, no, no, no, no, no, no, no, no, no, no, no, no, no, no, no, no, no, no. O'Neill.

When he worked for the *Baltimore Sun,* H. L. Mencken wrote an editorial that took up an entire page in the newspaper and consisted of a typeset "." repeated one million times. Mencken added a note that each dot represented someone who worked for the federal government.

Leon Bamberger, a movie studio executive, was the featured speaker at a Monday luncheon. When he paused during his lengthy speech, he heard a man at the head table ask his companion, "What follows Bamberger?"

"Wednesday," his friend explained.

In the 1950s, conservative members of the Texas legislature proposed a resolution honoring red-baiter Joseph McCarthy, inviting him to deliver a speech.

One daring representative, with the true-Texan name of Maury Maverick, introduced an amendment to the resolution that substituted Mickey Mouse for McCarthy, under the theory that if Texas wanted a rat, it should get a good rat.

English Prime Minister David Lloyd George offered to help explorer Ernest Shackleton raise money for an Antarctic expedition by introducing him to a millionaire who might finance the venture.

"Your friend offered me ten thousand pounds for my expenses," Shackleton reported back to the politician, "provided I would take you along with me to the pole. And he promised me one million pounds if I were to leave you there by mistake."

Movie actor Charles Laughton felt trapped at a dinner party when pianist Arthur Rubinstein insisted on showing home movies of his children engaged in backyard theatrics.

When the torture finally ended and the lights came back on, the actor told the concert pianist, "I've always regretted that I never had children. Because if I did, Mr. Rubinstein, I'd make them play the piano for you."

Writer Oscar Wilde did not think much of the American breed of intellectual. When American journalist Richard Harding Davis visited London, he met Wilde at a dinner. The Irish wit set the bait by asking Davis his opinion of French art.

The reporter thought he had dodged the setup, saying, "I never talk about things when I don't know the facts."

But Wilde had him hooked and reeled him in. "That must limit your conversation frightfully," he said.

Two wealthy women, one from Chicago, the other a proper Bostonian, were chatting at a luncheon. "In Boston," the easterner said, "we place all our emphasis on breeding."

"In Chicago," her companion said, "we also think it's great fun. But we do manage to foster a great many outside interests."

PAINTER JAMES MCNEILL WHISTLER:
"I CAN'T TELL YOU IF GENIUS IS HEREDITARY,
BECAUSE HEAVEN HAS GRANTED ME
NO OFFSPRING."

THIRTEEN

IMAGINARY PEBBLES AND PET LOBSTERS: THE WEIRD HABITS OF HIGHLY STRANGE PEOPLE

When I play shortstop, every inning I pick a pebble off the field and toss it away. That's the bad hop I won't get. If the infield is smooth, I toss away an imaginary pebble. And that's only weird habit No. 72 on my list. Am I the only person who, if it weren't for weird habits, would have no habits at all?

While thinking about his studies, Oxford scholar Gilbert Murray would pace his office, taking precisely seven steps before changing directions, then another seven steps, turn and repeat this pattern over and over again.

Concerned that his odd habit was a sign of a serious mental problem, Murray discussed it with a psychology professor, who dismissed the quirk as unimportant, but added this caution: "When you find yourself getting into multiples of seven, come see me again."

Menelik II, emperor of Ethiopia in the early 1900s, developed his own system of royal medicine. When he was ill, he ate several pages from the Bible, believing the book's holiness would cure him of any disease.

When he suffered a stroke in 1913, Menelik self-prescribed the Book of Kings for his recovery. The worse he felt, the more pages he ate. Either he ate too many or he didn't eat enough, because he died.

Gerard de Nerval was a notorious nineteenth-century poet. In Paris he could be seen strolling through the Palais-Royal gardens walking his pet lobster on a leash. Lobsters make better pets than dogs, the writer explained, because they do not bark.

When he was eighty-nine years old, the French orchestra conductor Pierre Monteux was asked what his remaining passions were in life.

"Two," he replied, "my model railway and women. But at the age of eighty-nine, I find I am getting a little too old for model railways."

Fame often gives people license to indulge their odd behaviors. Florence Nightingale, the Lady with the Lamp, devoted her life to tending the sick in hospitals, particularly wounded soldiers. But mercy doesn't preclude eccentricity.

When Nightingale made the rounds of the hospital wards, she carried a pet owl in her pocket. When the owl died, Nightingale had it stuffed and kept it in her pocket.

> SEVENTEENTH-CENTURY POET JOHN DONNE
> KEPT A COFFIN IN HIS WRITING ROOM AND
> WOULD CLIMB INSIDE TO REMIND HIMSELF
> HOW TEMPORARY IS LIFE.

Everyone eats dinner (if they're lucky), but some people do it differently:

1) The French painter Henri de Toulouse-Lautrec, a gourmet with original ideas, claimed that to have the best chicken for dinner you had to begin by chasing the bird with a gun until the animal was in a panic. Fright, Toulouse-Lautrec maintained, tenderized the chicken.

2) Another French gourmet, the novelist Alexander Dumas, advised that before you cook your poultry, you asphyxiate it in vinegar. "Violent death improves their flesh," he claimed.

Leave it to the French to invent the sport of extreme cooking.

3) Like a little ketchup on your ketchup? You'd have to go to some length to match Dustin Phillips, who went on the *Guinness World Records: Primetime* TV show in 1999 and sucked up an entire bottle of ketchup through a straw in only thirty-three seconds.

4) Business tycoon John Jacob Astor ate his ice cream with a knife—an interesting eccentricity and a tricky turn of the cutlery.

5) It wasn't the way he cooked his food that set writer Jonathan Swift apart, but the way he ate while pacing around his house. Swift believed the exercise he got by walking would cancel out the weight he put on by eating.

Nudity is not necessarily a habit, but it does have some extraordinary moments:

1) Sharon Mitchell, a star of X-rated movies, also posed for men's magazines. While trying to cash a check at the bank, she was

asked for identification. Mitchell didn't have her driver's license with her, but she did have a magazine in which she was prominently featured.

So she took off her shirt and struck the same magazine pose. The bank clerk accepted Mitchell's unusual form of identification and cashed the check.

2) Here's an idea the Department of Homeland Security might want to consider. In 2004 a New Jersey-based nudist magazine called *Travel Naturally* recommended that nudists help make America safer by whatever means were at hand.

All American women, the magazine suggested, should leave their houses totally naked. Why?

"It is a sin for a Taliban male to see any woman other than his wife naked," the magazine explained. "He must commit suicide if he does (which could explain the rash of suicide bombers around the world)."

3) A conceited actress well past her prime confided to the French priest Arthur Mugnier that she liked to gaze at herself naked in the mirror. "Is that a sin?" she asked.

"No, madam," the priest replied, "it is an error."

4) In Hollywood the naked look is part of the product design. You know how movie stars swear they wouldn't appear naked on the screen unless it was essential to artistic expression or their role in the movie?

British actress Helen Mirren told the truth behind that PR. "The part never calls for it," she said. "And I've never ever used that excuse. The box office calls for it."

5) "I never gave permission for the nudity in my movie, *Internal Affairs*," actress Nancy Travis said. "Sometimes, where they tell you the camera is pointed is not where it's pointed when you see the film. The important thing to them is making the movie. No one really cares about your welfare."

6) In the Western *Posse*, actress Salli Richardson found herself in the unusual position of shooting a naked love scene with the film's star, Mario Van Peebles, who also directed the movie.

Richardson saw an unusual advantage to the arrangement: "It makes one less man in the room."

7) On David Letterman's birthday, Drew Barrymore was a guest on his TV show. She forgot to bring him a gift, so the movie star stepped onto his desk, turned her back to the camera, and flashed her breasts at the host.

8) In Germany in 1853 a statue of Venus de Milo was arrested for public nudity. The artist being dead for several centuries, the statue itself was tried and convicted.

When Christopher Columbus discovered Cuba on his first voyage to the New World, the men on that island were already smoking cigars. But not like other smokers. The Cubans inhaled the smoke, not through their mouths, but by inserting the end of the cigar into their noses.

When King Farouk I of Egypt was overthrown in 1952, he had to flee the royal palace so quickly that he left behind most of his personal collections, including fifty canes, seventy-five pairs of binoculars, and one thousand neckties.

I can see that a man would need fifty canes, because you can never be too careful. But exactly how many binoculars could one person possibly use? If he was an avid bird-watcher, the king wouldn't have to suffer the shame of re-using the same binoculars for two and a half months. And if he dressed formally while out in the woods, he wouldn't appear in the same tie for three years. But tongues would wag when every sixth week he would be caught strolling with the same walking stick.

Styles change. What's out of fashion one year may be in the next—except for the people who have a style all their own because no one else wants it.

1) Demosthenes of ancient Greece devoted himself to his studies in an effort to become a scholar. Like many students before and since, he was tempted from his studies by the nightlife of Athens.

To discipline himself, Demosthenes grew his hair long and then shaved one side of his head, leaving the other side shaggy.

Too embarrassed by his bizarre appearance to show himself in public, he kept to his studies and became one of the most brilliant—and strangest looking—scholars of the ancient world.

2) Another practitioner of the halfway look, but with a different motive: the composer Frédéric Chopin.

While on tour as a concert pianist, Chopin took to shaving the right side of his face but let his beard grow on the left. Why? Because when he performed, the audience only saw him from the right profile.

3) Among the English elite in the early nineteenth century, gentlemen shaved off their own hair and donned elaborate wigs. The most famous diarist of the times, Samuel Pepys, came up with an interesting twist on this style. He cut off all his own hair, had it made into a wig, and wore that.

The English poet Samuel Taylor Coleridge had a brilliant mind and a weird wardrobe. While walking with a wealthy friend, Coleridge offered to step back if they encountered anyone of social standing, so the man could pass him off as a servant.

"Nonsense," his upper-class friend said. "I am proud of you as a friend. But I should be ashamed of you as a servant."

A nineteenth-century professor of medicine, Ernest Nebel of Germany, preferred dirty shirts to clean ones but realized that university administrators would frown upon his dirty little secret.

His solution: he wore several dirty shirts to his classes, one on top of the other, then topped them off with a clean shirt.

> BILLIONAIRE HOWARD HUGHES HAD AN EYE FOR DETAIL. THAT'S WHY HE DECREED THAT HIS CABINET DOORS WERE TO BE OPENED BY SERVANTS USING A MINIMUM OF FIFTEEN KLEENEXES PER DOOR, PER OPENING.

O ur own fears and obsessions seem perfectly normal because we have nurtured them for so long. But other people are just plain nuts.

Take the fourteenth-century French King Charles VI, who thought he was made of glass and was in constant danger of shattering.

N apoleon feared no man and no army, not even the Russians, although he would have been wise to be wary of Russians in winter. But the French leader did have a morbid fear of cats. So did the French King Henry III.

A German turkey farmer fashioned hundreds of tiny turbans and strapped them to the heads of his turkeys.

R at breeding is a popular hobby in both Japan and England. Pet owners brush their rats' fur with toothbrushes to get them ready for rat competitions.

Rat breeding has also proven popular with rats.

I t's Valentine's Day and you've come up with nothing? Not to worry. No present at all is better than a gift from Victor Emmanuel II, a nineteenth-century Italian king.

Once a year his highness presented to his favorite mistress the trimmed nail from his big toe. First, the nail was clipped by the servant in charge of the royal toes. Then a jeweler fashioned the nail into a gem setting, adorned with a gold edge and tiny diamonds.

And you've been throwing yours away.

T oenail fixations may be a guilty secret of the royal bloodlines. Edward James, the illegitimate son of King Edward VII, grew his toenails long, ten inches long, and had to walk on crutches.

When Wayne Gretzky was the world's greatest hockey player, he followed the same routine to get ready for each game. Before a game, he drank a Diet Coke, then a glass of water, Gatorade, another Diet Coke, and more Gatorade—then ate four hot dogs. Warming up on the ice, he always shot his first puck wide left. And it all worked—for him.

When Arizona Diamondbacks outfielder Luis Gonzalez and his wife had triplets, he developed the habit of tapping the plate three times with his bat every time he went up to hit.

Gonzalez also sent his bats to church, an approach to hitting he developed when playing for the Houston Astros. On the last day of the 1993 season, Gonzalez was hitting .299, one point from the magical .300 plateau.

Teammates were attending a chapel service in the clubhouse. Gonzales got the inspiration to put his bats in a room full of prayers, asking them to return the bats when they were done.

"It worked," Gonzales said. "I got a hit that day and ended up hitting .300 on the dot."

Some fans may think that God has other things to take care of besides bats, but no one in the game argues religion with a .300 hitter.

FOURTEEN

REDESIGNING THE SKY: TWISTED EGOS OF THE STARS

British rocker Marc Almond got the ratio of fame to vacuity right when he said, "Five minutes of stardom means another sixty-five years of emptiness."

That's a deal many people would take. But if you're going to become a celebrity, make sure you've got the inflatable ego first.

Painter James McNeill Whistler had the talent of a genius and the ego to match. While taking in the night sky with a friend, he gazed at the stars and said, "I would have done it differently."

Movie fans aren't the only people who get surprised on Oscar night. Consider what happened to these winners:

1) Director John Avildsen: "I had no idea *Rocky* would be such a hit. I thought it was going to be the second half of a double bill at a drive-in."

2) Actress Shirley Jones: "After I won the Oscar, my salary doubled, my friends tripled, my kids became more popular at school, the butcher made a pass at me, and my maid asked for a raise."

3) Actress Jane Fonda: "Movie stars are people's heroes, heroines. It's so much a central part of our culture, and this is the night that one of them might fall down."

4) Actress Sally Field: "When I won for *Norma Rae*, all I could think about was I was going to fall down, I'm going to humiliate myself."

5) Actor Gary Busey: "Oscar night is just another excuse to get drunk."

6) Actor Richard Dreyfuss: "It deserves every negative, sarcastic thing ever said about it, and it's also one of the greatest evenings of your life."

Even the pets of the stars are special. Some people tire of hearing their talking parrot say the same thing over and over again. Not artist Paul Cézanne. He taught his parrot to say the only words he wanted to hear: "Cézanne is a great painter."

Great players can make lousy teammates. Infielder Billy Werber once asked Joe DiMaggio's teammate Charlie Keller what the great Yankee center fielder was really like.

"I can't say," Keller replied. "The man never said a word to me." Keller and DiMaggio were teammates for eight years.

AH, THE RICH: FREDERICK THE GREAT OF PRUSSIA LOVED HIS COFFEE, BUT HIS COFFEE WAS NOT YOUR COFFEE OR MINE. HIS COFFEE WAS BREWED WITH CHAMPAGNE INSTEAD OF SOMETHING SO COMMON AS WATER.

Millionaire gambler Diamond Jim Brady was notorious for his huge appetite, which matched his extravagant generosity. He made a fortune and spent it all on wine, women, and more wine and women.

When Brady died, one of his favorite restaurateurs, Charles Rector, mourned, "I have lost my four best customers."

Three signs of the artistic temperament:
1) Poet Edith Sitwell: "I have often wished I had time to cultivate modesty. But I am too busy thinking about myself."

2) Writer Anatole France: "A writer is rarely so well inspired as when he talks about himself."

3) Painter Pablo Picasso: "If I spit, they will take my spit and frame it as great art."

Hollywood's most unusual actress, Parker Posey, prefers to play off-the-wall, over-the-edge characters, a specialty she's done to perfection in such movies as *The House of Yes, Party Girl, Kicking and Screaming,* and *The Doom Generation.*

Mark Waters directed Parker in *The House of Yes,* in which she plays a woman who's convinced she is Jacqueline Kennedy. "Parker isn't the girl next door," Walters said, "unless you're living next door to the Addams Family."

"I do feel crazy at times," Posey admitted. "But that's normal. I think the people you should worry about are the ones who say, 'Everything is fine.'"

Sometimes celebrities say more about themselves than they think they're saying.

1) Actor Warren Beatty: "Charity is taking an ugly girl to lunch."

2) TV personality Bryant Gumbel: "It's not that I dislike many people. It's just that I don't like many people."

3) Movie star Sylvester Stallone: "I'm the Hiroshima of love."

4) Actor John Travolta: "If I'm androgynous, I'd say I lean towards macho-androgynous."

How would you like to work for a Hollywood legend who does what you do, only better? It happened to writer Douglas McGrath, who had written a novel and essays but not movies.

However, McGrath did have a girlfriend (he was later smart enough to marry) who worked for Woody Allen. One day Allen asked her, "Do you think Doug would like to collaborate on a screenplay with me?"

"After I woke up in the hospital from shock, I said yes," McGrath recalled. He quickly found himself working with Allen on the script for what became the movie comedy *Bullets Over Broadway*.

"Whenever he has an idea, Woody snaps the fingers on both hands, then acts out the idea," McGrath said. "But I couldn't concentrate on anything he was saying. He would finish an idea and ask, 'What do you think?'"

McGrath's problem: He was so in awe of working with Woody Allen that he "hadn't heard one word he'd said." McGrath quickly worked out a system of comic survival. Whenever Allen tried out a joke on him, McGrath would nod thoughtfully and say, "Maybe, maybe."

It worked. "I think he thought that meant I was very discriminating," recalled McGrath, who convinced enough Hollywood people that he knew what he was doing to let him direct Gwyneth Paltrow in his film version of *Emma*.

Hollywood directors usually get what they want from actors, if they're clever at manipulating their stars' egos. In the comedy *It Happened One Night*, director Frank Capra wanted star Claudette Colbert to lift her skirt as she demonstrated to Clark Gable the most effective way for a hitchhiker to stop a car.

Colbert refused to do the scene, considering the peek immodest. Capra told his star he would bring in a chorus girl and shoot her legs instead. Colbert changed her mind and did the scene, so word wouldn't get around Hollywood that her legs needed doubling.

It Happened One Night went on to win the Oscar for Best Picture and Colbert was named Best Actress, legs and all.

The tricky part of surviving in Hollywood is that every time you get their tricks figured out, they pull a new one on you.

Take this lesson learned the hard way by two young producers, husband-and-wife team Julia and Michael Phillips, who made the Robert Redford/Paul Newman hit, *The Sting*. The Phillipses thought their contract assured them equal producing credits by guaranteeing that when their names appeared on the screen, the letters would be equal in height with executive producers Richard Zanuck and David Brown.

But Zanuck and Brown were Hollywood veterans. The junior producers got outfoxed when the credits rolled. The Phillipses found their names were smaller on the screen. Why? They had won equal letter height, but they had failed to negotiate for the all-important equal letter width.

When Pat Nixon was the nation's First Lady, she was named Macaroni Woman of the Year by the American Macaroni Institute. Well, who else would give her that award? As part of the honor, Pat was sculpted in pasta.

What the institute never made public was who Pat beat out for the honors. How would you feel coming in second in a macaroni contest?

Actors need selfishness to survive the system and selflessness to portray other people. "When I started going out on auditions, they kept saying to me, 'Just be yourself,'" Annette Bening recalled. "And I would think: Now how do I do that?"

The people who run Hollywood were unmercifully needled in director Robert Altman's *The Player,* a satiric dissection of the movie industry.

After the film became a hit, Altman expected to feel the wrath of the rich and powerful studio execs he ridiculed in the movie. But it never happened. "All the bad stuff about Hollywood in the movie," Altman said, "they figured I was talking about the other guy."

When Chauncey Leopardi was eleven, he became a child star in Hollywood by landing a role in *The Sandlot*. His sudden celebrity gave the boy a chance to meet his favorite stars, including comic actor Steve Martin.

"You would think it's all comedy for Steve," Leopardi said. "But he's very serious about his work." Chauncey asked Martin for his autograph. "He handed me a card that had his autograph already printed on it," the boy said.

What's it take to become a major Hollywood producer? Discriminating judgment.

"When I was in the fifth grade, my mother bought me a pair of Wrangler jeans instead of Levi's," *Top Gun* producer Don Simpson recalled. "I said, 'I'll stay in my room rather than wear those things. If you don't understand the difference, you don't understand anything.' And I won. I never wore those jeans. I care a lot about aesthetics."

When the action movie *The Last Action Hero* opened in 1993, Columbia Pictures contracted to pay NASA $50,000 to paint Arnold Schwarzenegger's picture on the side of a rocket being launched into space that summer.

Columbia was chosen for the first ad-in-space for "their ingenious creativity that represents the same goals as the American space program," according to Mike Lawson, head of Space Marketing Inc.

You may have thought that the American space program had something to do with boldly exploring the cosmos. Apparently, NASA's goals were to make Arnie even richer than he already was and to make sure that if we meet an alien race from outer space, it has a good grasp of our values.

The ad program was canceled shortly before blast-off.

We all know that celebrities get treated better than ordinary people. Star worship has become so automatic in America, we assume preferential treatment is a basic right of the stars—life, liberty, and the pursuit of fame. But celebrities get the benefit of the doubt in surprising ways.

Babe Ruth was such a big star that when a policeman found the Yankee slugger trying to start his car while drunk, he offered to help. Ruth got mad when the officer suggested that he shouldn't drive, and the Babe slugged the cop.

Instead of arresting Ruth, the policeman got back up, started his car, and drove the slugger home. Not many of us are going to get that kind of treatment.

When an Israeli policeman stopped Moshe Dayan for speeding, the general had an interesting excuse. Dayan, blind in one eye, always wore an eye patch. "I've only got one eye," he explained to the officer. "What do you want me to watch: the speedometer or the road?"

A reporter asked the aging stage and screen star John Barrymore if acting was as much fun as it used to be. Barrymore cut him down with a great response: "Young man, I am seventy-five. Nothing is as much fun as it used to be."

It wasn't considered draft dodging during the Civil War when wealthy men paid substitutes to take their place in the Union Army.

Many of the wealthy class, then as now, felt they could help the fighting best by letting other people do it.

When Grover Cleveland ran for president in 1884, his advisers worried that his adversaries would call him a draft dodger for having bought his way out of the Civil War.

Their problem was eliminated when they found out that Cleveland's opponent, James Blaine, had also paid someone else to fight for him. Evasion of duty never became an issue in that campaign, because both candidates wanted to evade the question.

The hiring of substitutes to do what the rich expect the poor to do for themselves is a time-honored privilege that the rich extend to themselves.

Catherine de Medici, before she became queen of France in the sixteenth century, hired a substitute pilgrim to make a journey from France to Jerusalem to fulfill a promise she'd made to God.

Nothing unusual in a member of the ruling class using someone else to appease God. What was unusual: his prescribed method of travel. The pilgrim was required to travel on foot, three steps forward, one step back—all the way.

When movie star Robert Redford began directing films, the studios offered him major stars for his pictures. But Redford turned them down, preferring to work with relatively unknown actors. He chose Timothy Hutton for *Ordinary People*, Daniel Stern and Rubén Blades for *The Milagro Beanfield War*, and a then little-known Brad Pitt for *A River Runs Through It*.

Redford explained his directorial method: "Working with

unknowns puts the emphasis on the character without people being distracted by having someone like me in the movie."

T he French woman writer with the man's name, George Sand, was a close friend of Hungarian composer Franz Liszt. The two liked to work together—Sand writing her novels, while Liszt scored his compositions—sitting at opposite ends of a long table in her Parisian home.

Because of Sand's notoriety for turning friends and artists into lovers, Parisian bohemia assumed she was having an affair with Liszt.

Sand denied it. "Liszt loves no one but God and the Holy Virgin," George proclaimed, "who does not resemble me in the slightest degree."

F rank Sinatra had a hit in 1942 with a weird novelty song called *They've Got an Awful Lot of Coffee in Brazil.* It became such an expected part of his nightclub act that Sinatra would walk on stage carrying a coffee cup and receive a standing ovation.

How many people in history have ever heard the cheers of the crowd for drinking coffee?

V eteran actress Maureen O'Hara stayed out of movies for twenty years and then decided to make her big comeback in a terrible comedy called *Only the Lonely.* The movie bombed; so did her second career.

WRITER JOHN LE CARRÉ MADE A LOT OF MONEY
SELLING HIS SPY NOVELS TO FILM STUDIOS, EVEN
IF HE DIDN'T THINK MUCH OF THE RESULTS THAT
WERE PUT UP ON THE SCREEN. "HAVING YOUR
BOOK TURNED INTO A MOVIE," HE SAID, "IS LIKE
SEEING YOUR OXEN BECOME BOUILLON CUBES."

FIFTEEN

ON TO PARADISE: HIDDEN MEANINGS AND ODD ORIGINS

In ancient times, if a clan decided to get rid of someone who was causing them too much trouble, they burned down his house.

We don't do as much of that as we used to. When we say someone got fired from a job, we're invoking that ancient image of burning as a form of rejection.

By the time something becomes common knowledge, its origin has been obscured. That's why many of the wackiest stories start at the beginning.

What grows on cacao trees? Cocoa beans? Shouldn't that be cocoa trees or cacao beans—consistent one way or the other?

The English language has never been noted for its consistency. So when an English explorer brought cacao beans back to England, someone spelled it wrong in an official report. It's been cocoa ever since—another victory for the persistence of typos.

According to the *Oxford English Dictionary*, more than three hundred words in the English language started out as typos.

So if you find any typos in this book, leave them alone. We're trying to get into the OED.

"**J**ack, be nimble. Jack, be quick. Jack, jump over the candlestick." Why was so much depending on Jack?

These instructions were not just a simple childhood diversion. Candlestick leaping was a test of your future, if you lived in medieval England.

If you were nimble and quick enough to leap the candle without blowing out the flame, that meant good luck for your future. Bad luck if you couldn't.

Successful jumping was a good-luck charm throughout Europe. In northern Spain, a village's young babies were placed on the ground, and a man, symbolizing the dangers infants face in life, leaped over them. If he landed without hurting one of the babies, that symbolized their safe passage through the early years.

Big ideas may start from the smallest motivations. In 1950 a businessman named Francis Xavier McNamara hosted a luncheon at a restaurant for some clients. When the bill arrived, McNamara was embarrassed to discover he'd left his cash in another pair of pants.

Vowing that would never happen again, McNamara threw out all his pants except for one pair.

Just kidding. He took the more sensible approach: he started the Diners Card, which launched the travel credit card industry.

THE ENGLISH USED TO SHOUT, "HUZZAH!" SOME STILL SHOUT, "HURRAH!" BOTH SHOUTS COME FROM THE BATTLE CRY OF NORSE WARRIORS, MEANING: "ON TO PARADISE!"

Late to work? Late for a date? Worried all the time about being on time? Blame it on the railroads.

In the 1800s precise time just wasn't that important. Most people lived by the sun, and most towns kept their own time based on when the sun was overhead.

That solar clock appeared overhead at a slightly different time from place to place. As a result, there were hundreds of noons across America.

The multiplicity of time made it impossible to run trains on schedule because no one agreed what the time was. Looking at the problem another way, the trains may have run on time, but the people who wanted to ride didn't.

Riders would miss their trains, because the railroad companies' concept of noon was completely different than the passengers'. The railroads couldn't make up a schedule for all the stops along their route, because each station was running on a different time.

So in 1883 the railroad companies got together and adopted a standard time, with four time zones for the whole country. Nearly all of us have been late ever since.

You may see coconut palms on islands and along coastlines around the world. That's because when coconuts fall into the ocean, they don't sink. They float. The nuts may drift for thousands of miles. When they wash ashore, they take root almost anywhere.

This is a tree that travels and spreads in a relaxed yet successful fashion, kind of like beach bums, the coconuts of the human race.

You know how the parking patrol chalks tires to make sure you don't park too long in city garages? That idea came from an old army procedure, which also led to a second, completely different tradition.

Back in the seventeenth century, army officers would make beer checks of the camp each night. They'd tap the bungs back into the beer kegs at the end of day and then chalk them. In the morning, they'd check the chalk marks to make sure soldiers hadn't raided the kegs for more beer after lights out.

The chalk-and-tap technique inspired not only Rita the meter maid, but also the army custom of blowing taps on the bugle at close of day.

Speaking of the army, how did the military salute begin? Not on a battlefield and not exactly from military tradition.

The salute dates back to 1588 when Admiral Francis Drake surprised everyone by defeating the mighty Spanish Armada. England's Queen Elizabeth came to the docks to congratulate the sailors.

A naval officer, whose name has been lost to the ages, ordered the men to shield their eyes with their right hands "on account of the dazzling loveliness of Her Majesty."

Now that's the art of diplomacy.

We see a ship flying the skull and crossbones, and we know what that means: pirates, the scourge of the seven seas. But it didn't start out that way.

Captains of lawful ships hoisted the skull and crossbones to warn other ships that they had a contagious disease aboard. Pirates adopted the flag as a ruse to keep their many enemies away from their loot-laden ships. Pirate ships originally flew a plain red flag or nothing at all.

Ever hear of Rollow the Red-Nosed Reindeer? How about Reginald with his nose so bright?

Those were the first names dreamed up by ad man Robert May when he invented Santa's most famous flying reindeer for a Montgomery Ward Christmas advertising flyer.

Generations of kids were saved from having Reginald the Red-Nosed Reindeer go down in history when May's four-year-old daughter chose Rudolph instead.

In 1892 an odd song, *Ta-ra-ra-boom-der-e,* became a big hit in England and the United States. In the 1950s, the song, credited to Henry Sayers, provided the melody for the theme song of a popular kids' TV show, *Howdy Doody.*

Sayers later admitted he hadn't written the melody. He'd adapted it from a tune he'd heard played in a brothel in St. Louis. Howdy, kids.

All cultures develop myths and theories to explain how the world was created. Some theorists even know exactly when the deed was done:

James Ussher, the Irish archbishop of Armagh, wrote in 1650 that the world "was created on 22nd October, 4004 B.C., at 6 o'clock in the evening."

In 1859 John Lightfoot, vice chancellor of the University of

Cambridge, recalculated Ussher's research and declared that the world was actually created on "the twenty-third of October, 4004 B.C., at nine o'clock in the morning."

I think we've missed a good bet for a two-day holiday: World Creation Days, October 22–23.

Why do the knives we use for dinner have rounded tips? It's not a matter of style but of manners.

French King Louis XIV issued a royal decree that banned table knives with pointed ends, because he was sick of watching slovenly eaters pick their teeth with their knives.

Coming up with movie titles can be a tricky business. When director Alan Taylor was in production on the crime comedy *Palookaville,* the film's working title was *One for the Money.*

"I thought that was the most boring title in the world," Taylor said. "One day I was talking with the producer and he asked, 'Come up with a new title yet?'"

Taylor had. "But it was ridiculous," he recalled, "and had no connection with the movie. I didn't want to tell him."

On his own, the producer had thought of a new title too, which "he didn't want to tell me either," Taylor said.

Both director and producer had come up with the same ridiculous title, *Palookaville*. "So we felt we had to keep it," Taylor said. And they did.

The exalted may have surprisingly humble origins. Da Vinci's Mona Lisa was a commissioned portrait, paid for by King Francis I of France.

What did the king do when the great artist delivered one of the world's masterpieces? He hung it in his bathroom.

Scholars who devised medieval calendars described two days of each month as "evil days." On these days, people expected the worst, knowing nothing good would happen. These two days were called the "dies mali," from which we get the word "dismal."

Ever been to the Desert Desert? Sounds redundant, but so does the Sahara Desert, since "sahara" means "desert" in Arabic.

The other place that's so arid they said it twice is the Gobi Desert. Yep, in Mongolian, "gobi" means "desert."

Odd origins of common things:

1) Our handy Kleenex, without which kids would be a drippy mess, was first manufactured as gas mask filters during World War I.

2) Everyone's toy chest contains an old yo-yo, probably with its string in knots. The toy was first used as a weapon by hunters in the Philippines, who figured that if you threw a rock at a target and missed, you had to go pick up the rock or find another one. Why waste all that effort?

   Instead, yo-yo wielding hunters lurked in trees, waiting for an unsuspecting rabbit to hop along below. A hunter would spin down the yo-yo and knock the rabbit on the head. If he missed, the hunter didn't have to climb down the tree to retrieve his weapon. He snapped the two-way rock back up and waited for the next rabbit.

3) In 1847 a fifteen-year-old boy sitting in his mother's kitchen complained because the center of his fried cake was soggy with grease.

   Other boys had complained about soggy cakes before, but Hanson Gregory of Maine decided to do something about it. He poked out the center of some cakes with a fork before they were fried.

   After his mother fried up the funny-looking cakes with the holes in the middle, young Gregory had done the world a great service: he had invented the doughnut. The rest is good eating.

Gregory, by the way, went on to become the doughnut-eating captain of a Yankee clipper ship.

Where does greatness come from? And misery, does it bear any relationship to greatness?

"Every king springs from a race of slaves," the Greek philosopher Plato observed, "and every slave has had kings among his ancestors."

Civilization: a mighty achievement of mankind? Or an attempt to get dates?

"If there hadn't been women, we'd still be squatting in a cave eating raw meat," filmmaker Orson Welles said. "We made civilization in order to impress our girlfriends."

ACTRESS JOANNE WOODWARD: "MY MIDDLE NAME IS GIGNILLIAT, BUT I WAS NAMED FOR JOAN CRAWFORD. IN THE SOUTH, CRAWFORD WAS REVERED, AND HER NAME WAS PRONOUNCED 'JO-ANNE.'"

Some things that start off very small grow enough to change the course of history.

The next time you're flying on a Boeing 707, look out the window at the plane's wingspan. The Wright Brothers' first successful flight did not stay in the air long enough to span the wings of the plane in which you can now fly around the world.

If you've ever been to Plymouth Rock in Massachusetts, you may have asked that obvious visitor question: Why did the Pilgrims land here? Not the easiest landing, not the most hospitable shore, and Plymouth Rock is too small for anyone to stand on.

Why didn't the voyagers on the *Mayflower* continue south until they found a more promising shoreline? A clue appears in the diary of one of America's first colonists: The ship was out of beer; low on food too, but out of beer was the first consideration.

Why did Christopher Columbus take along Jewish interpreters on his exploratory voyage to the New World?

He reasoned that the people he would meet in the New World would be ancient and, therefore, they'd speak Hebrew.

A LAW IN ANCIENT ROME ORDERED PROSTITUTES
TO WEAR YELLOW WIGS, WHICH MADE IT EASIER
FOR GUYS TO KNOW WHERE TO GO FOR A DATE. IT
ALSO RUINED THE REPUTATION OF BLONDES FOR
GENERATIONS TO COME.

In the twelfth century the Catholic Church condemned cats as "ambassadors of the devil" and initiated a program to eradicate cats throughout Europe. Cats were slaughtered, and defiant cat-lovers were burned at the stake as witches.

The chief beneficiary of this anti-cat policy was the rat population of Europe. Their increased numbers spread the Black Plague, since there were not enough cats to control the rats. Millions of people died. Then the church changed its mind.

❧ SIXTEEN ❧

INSIDE HOLLYWEIRD: BEHIND THE SCENES IN LA-LA LAND

Trying to figure out if you have what it takes to make it in Holly-wood? You might try talent, desire, beauty, hard work.

Or you could take the approach of movie director Myles Berkowitz, who broke in three ways at once: as star, director, and writer of his first film, *20 Dates*.

"I never thought I had such amazing talent," Berkowitz said. "But I knew that a lot of people who were making it didn't either. There's so much non-talent out there, I couldn't understand why I couldn't be one of them."

The Oscars mean red carpets, golden statues, and a lot of flashy eye makeup. But it's not all glamour and glitz. Actually, it is all glamour and glitz. Plus, a few wacky moments.

1) What did it mean for Mercedes Ruehl to win an Oscar for Best Supporting Actress for *The Fisher King* in 1991?

"I shall never waitress again," Ruehl swore, "and you are my witnesses."

2) Barry Fitzgerald was named Best Supporting Actor for *Going My Way* in 1944. One day while practicing his golf swing indoors, he drove the head right off Oscar. Paramount paid for a replacement.

3) In 1982 Zbigniew Rybezynski won an Oscar for the Best Animated Short Film, then stepped outside the auditorium for a cigarette.

When the Polish filmmaker tried to get back inside, security guards thought he was a gatecrasher. He spoke no English and couldn't find his ticket. So Rybezynski became the only Oscar winner (so far) to celebrate his victory by spending the night in jail.

Toy Story became a huge hit for an animated movie. But when the producers were trying to line up the rights to use toys in the film, they couldn't land one of their favorites: GI Joe.

"The company executives didn't want us inspiring kids to blow up GI Joe," recalled Andrew Stanton, who wrote *Toy Story*.

"We tried to point out to them that if boys blew up their GI Joes, they'd have to buy new ones."

It didn't work, and the producers had to settle for little green army men instead, which led to a casting oddity: the sergeant in *Toy Story* was played by R. Lee Ermey, a former Marine drill instructor who played the same role in the Vietnam War drama *Full Metal Jacket*.

Composer Marvin Hamlisch was hired to write the music for the movie *Frankie & Johnny*, about an offbeat romance between a short-order cook (Al Pacino) and a waitress (Michelle Pfeiffer).

A studio exec told Hamlisch not to make the music big, because Pfeiffer and Pacino were playing poor people.

The movie's director Garry Marshall recalled Hamlisch's response: "When poor people are in love, what do you think they hear—accordions? Don't be crazy. Poor people have music in their hearts too. They hear violins just like rich people."

Mark Gill, a Hollywood exec, explained why there is greater satisfaction in successfully promoting a bad movie than a good one. "It doesn't matter if the movie doesn't deliver," he told *Harper's* magazine. "If you can create the impression that the movie delivers, you're fine. That's the difference between playability and marketability.

"If a movie opens big and then crashes, that's when you know that the marketing campaign was absolute perfection."

Two views of what goes wrong in Hollywood from industry insiders who've seen it happen too many times:

1) Director Bryan Forbes, who made the small masterpiece *Whistle Down the Wind*, wanted to write original screenplays for his films but found the movie studios unreceptive.

    "The trouble is that those who run our industry hate to back a horse until it has gone past the winning post," he said. "Since there is little evidence to suggest that many of them can actually read, they prefer to have something in hard covers that they can, at least, weigh."

2) Hollywood studios often change the director's cut of a film based on reactions they get from test audiences. That system creates more problems than it solves.

    "Most of the time, fixing the ending can't do the job, because most pictures aren't very good," film director Sidney Lumet wrote in his book, *Making Movies*. Lumet made several of Hollywood's best movies, including *The Verdict, Dog Day Afternoon,* and *Network*.

    The inherent value of a movie doesn't necessarily lead to success or failure. "Good pictures become hits," Lumet observed. "Good pictures become flops. Bad pictures make money. Bad pictures lose money. The fact is that no one really knows. If anyone did know, he'd be able to write his own ticket."

What makes one thing funny and another not? Let's turn to Billy Crystal for an answer — the actor who was funny as a stand-up, on TV, and in such movies as *City Slickers* and *When Harry Met Sally,* but not necessarily such movies as *Mr. Saturday Night* and *America's Sweethearts.*

In *City Slickers*, Crystal improvised through a funny scene of a phone call from his mother. He borrowed that moment from his own life. "My mother does call me on my birthday," he explained. "But she does it at 7:30 in the morning. I had to change the time to 5:17 in the movie, because 7:30 isn't funny; 5:17, now that's funny."

And he's right. Crystal stars in that film as a city boy on a cattle drive. He also produced *City Slickers* and almost decided to direct it himself.

What kept him from directing? "I didn't want to have to direct me and four hundred cows," he explained. "After a few days, the cows started to understand the director's instructions. They became method cows."

You know how most movie and TV characters live in the same phone prefix: 555-land?

When characters in a movie give out their phone number, it's always something like 555-1234 or 555-9876. The 555 prefix is the null number the phone company gives Hollywood so movie nuts won't call real people to see if Brad or Julia answers.

In the Michael Douglas thriller *The Game*, the filmmaker tried to get around the old 555 routine by having his actor say the phone number this way: "Fifty-five-five-six-seven-eight-nine."

Nice try.

Jim Varney played Ernest P. Worrell, the tool-challenged king of comedy, first in TV commercials and then in several movies. While Varney was a classically trained Shakespearean actor, he became so identified with the role of Ernest that he could predict Worrell's entire life.

In between films, Ernest devoted his time to "cross-breeding power tools," Varney said. "He's working on a belt sander and blender so you can sand the table top and make a milkshake at the same time."

Varney, who died in 2000, taking Ernest with him, predicted Ernest's parting words: "It's getting dark in here. Better check them fuses."

We all know you can't believe what you see in the movies. Often, you can't believe what you hear either.

1) For the buffalo stampede in the Western *Dances with Wolves*, sound-effects experts buried their microphones under half a foot of dirt. They then beat the ground with rocks, shoes packed with dirt, and coconuts. And that's what a herd of buffalo sounds like.

2) To create the submarine engines in the underwater thriller *The Hunt for Red October*, the sound experts used a Chevy for one sub and a Rolls Royce for another. The third sub was given a distinctive sound by mixing recordings of heavy machinery with the roars of panthers, the growls of bears, and the heartbeats of lions.

To produce the submarines' sonar pings, the sound crew worked their way through 120 different ping effects and came up with eight finalists. Two of the winning pings were rejected — not by the director but by the navy. The movie's pings were too close to sonar sounds the navy had classified as top secret.

3) In the thriller *The Pelican Brief*, John Heard gets shot, and his blood splatters noisily across a hot TV screen. How did the sound effects wizards achieve that gruesome sound? By recording the sound of bacon frying in a pan.

Movie director Steven Soderbergh had a surprise cult hit with his first film, the oddly titled *sex, lies, and videotape*. Soderbergh had used that only as a working title during production, intending to change it before the movie was released.

"It was almost a glib assessment of what the film was about," he said. "It was a mock title, like calling a film *Blood and Guts*. We thought that calling it *sex, lies, and videotape* would kill the movie."

But at an early test screening, the audience really liked the title because it was so unusual. "It became obvious that it would be stupid to change the title," Soderbergh said. "Also, no one could come up with an alternative."

Patrick Swayze was at the top of the Hollywood star machine after playing a sexy guy in *Dirty Dancing,* a tough guy in *Red Dawn,* and a romantic guy in *Ghost.* Then he made the strangest career choices: playing a Zen hobo in *Three Wishes,* a drag queen in *To Wong Foo, Thanks for Everything! Julie Newmar,* and a doctor devoted to India's poor in *City of Joy.*

"I've lived through the hit machine mentality," Swayze said. "Now I'm having a great time screwing up my career. I feel very self-indulgent in this movie-star life.

"I thought about blowing this business off because it's devoid of humanness," he admitted. "It lacks dignity. I suppose now everyone will say I'm just this sensitive guy. I'd better make a movie where I kill something pretty soon."

After the surprise success of *Wong Foo,* Swayze considered doing a sequel, but said, "They would have to pay us a lot of money. Wesley (co-star in drag Wesley Snipes) took his wig and gowns and burned them after the shooting was over. As for me, it took me many years to grow six hairs on my chest, and I'm not going to shave them off again for nothing."

In 1992 filmmaker Woody Allen and actress Mia Farrow broke off their long relationship in a scandal over his affair with her adopted daughter.

When the scandal broke in the nation's press, Hollywood responded by moving up the release date of Allen's latest film (which co-starred Farrow), *Husbands and Wives*. The comic drama mirrored the real-life scandal, dealing, in part, with an older man (Allen) leaving his wife (Farrow) for a younger woman.

What was Hollywood's view of the scandal? Columnist Martin Grove wrote in the *Hollywood Reporter*, the movie industry trade journal: "What's really good about that coverage (of the scandal) is that it's mostly been on newspapers' front pages or in main news sections, rather than on the movie pages where it's hard to stand out."

> "I'M DELIGHTED WITH TELEVISION BECAUSE IT USED TO BE THAT FILMS WERE THE LOWEST FORM OF ART," MOVIE DIRECTOR BILLY WILDER SAID. "NOW WE'VE GOT SOMETHING TO LOOK DOWN UPON."

In Hollywood, reality never gets in the way of marketing.

In the wake of the bombing of the federal building in Oklahoma City, Hollywood thought it was a good time to release a little Chuck

Norris film called *Top Dog*, in which he fights militia-like terrorists who plot to overthrow the government by bombing buildings and killing kids.

Despite that dubious plot line, *Top Dog* was sold as a kids' comedy. Debra Stein, a marketing exec for the company that produced the movie, defended its scenes of people being shot, blown up, burned alive, tortured, punched, and kicked.

None of that, according to Stein, was violence.

"There's action in *Top Dog*," she explained. "I wouldn't call it violence."

R odd Wolff was a Hollywood stuntman who specialized in horse falls for dozens of movies and TV shows. How did he break into the falling end of the stunt business? Accidentally.

At nineteen he landed a bit part in an episode of the TV Western *Death Valley Days*. During the shooting, his horse fell by accident. Everyone on the set thought Wolff did the fall so well, they talked him into becoming a stuntman.

The most dangerous movie he ever fell in? *Rambo III*, with its battle scene of Afghan warriors fighting on horseback. In the middle of 750 mounted extras, Wolff and his horse did a dramatic fall in a cloud of dust.

"The second line of riders behind me were stuntmen to protect me," he explained. "But the riders behind them weren't stuntmen. I hoped they could see me, even though I couldn't see them. If one of their horses had stepped on my head, it would have been all over."

Wolff survived the film, but that's how close to the edge stuntmen can work. "It's amazing that no one was killed on that show," he said.

In his book *Vietnam at the Movies*, Vietnam veteran and author Michael Lee Lanning offered dim views of nearly all the Hollywood attempts to depict that war accurately.

About the infamous Russian roulette scene in *The Deer Hunter*, Lanning said: "There was no such thing as gambling on Russian roulette in Vietnam. If there was, the people would not surround the contestants, because bullets fired into the temple tend to come out the other side."

About *Platoon*, he said, "Everything that went wrong in the entire course of the war happens to that one platoon."

About the Rambo movies, Lanning scoffed: "Anyone who believes that Rambo could jump from a cliff onto rocks and receive a minor cut probably also believes that a club fighter named Rocky could go the distance with the world's heavyweight champion."

They do things differently in Hollywood, even if there's no particular reason for it. Let's say a producer sends someone to a costume shop to rent a costume for a film production. The producers pay for the rental differently than you or I would for the same costume.

On the first day, the producer pays one-tenth of the costume's purchase price. The second day, the rental is one-twentieth of the price. The third day is free. Then the cycle starts all over again and continues that way for as long as the movie is in production.

Why such a strange pricing system? It's been going on in Hollywood for so long that no one remembers why.

The Gregory Peck drama *To Kill a Mockingbird* won over generations of children and parents with its heartfelt message of family strength and honor.

But the movie almost never got made. Peck saved the film, according to Horton Foote, who wrote the screenplay for *Mockingbird*.

"Universal, the studio that made it, couldn't stand the film," Foote said. "But Gregory put in his contract that the director had final cut. So the studio couldn't touch it."

It's rare for a star to use his influence to protect the director's vision. "If the studio had gotten its hand on it," Foote said, "God knows what it would have turned out to be."

Many movies use a stunt double for the lead actor. In *White Fang*, the wolf cub star had eighteen doubles.

"You can't film with a cub for very long," wolf trainer Pam Buttler explained. "They're like little kids. You have to work around their napping schedule."

It takes equal amounts of patience and ingenuity to work with wolves. "You can't make a wolf do something that's not in its nature to do," Buttler said. "It took months to get a wolf to jump on a man."

To get the wolves to show anger, Buttler would hold a bone just off-camera and then snatch it away. The wolves would snarl at her and show their teeth till she gave the bone back.

For the fight scenes, the wolf cubs and dogs were actually playing. The fight sounds, added later, changed the appearance of what was happening on the screen.

SEVENTEEN

DRIVING IN TURKMENISTAN: THE ODDS AGAINST US

"All life is six to five against," the writer Damon Runyon pointed out seventy years ago.

The odds haven't improved since then. But we do invent strange ways to lose.

amiliarity breeds statistical ignorance. Scientists know so much more about the universe then they did previously that we now know how much we don't know, which is a lot more than we thought it was.

Physicists say that 90 percent of what exists in the universe is as yet unknown to us. We have a long way to go. Will we ever get there? Who knows?

Perhaps among that unknown 90 percent are discoveries that will turn things around, make us smarter, get us there faster, make everything we've discovered so far seem like ancient history.

E ver used the TV to babysit the kids? Perhaps you're the one parent in the USA who hasn't. Other people must be making up for your share, since the average American kid watches the tube three hours a day.

If you're a kid with the TV habit, all we can say is, "Turn on the tube and pass the cigs, fatso."

Researchers claim that the more TV kids watch, the higher their chances of becoming obese and turning into smokers when they grow up.

D oes old dad drive you nuts? It's not his fault.

Researchers claim that children whose fathers were old when they were born tend to suffer from more mental illness when they grow up than kids born to younger fathers.

T hen there are the things we probably could have figured out without the help of scientists. For example, researchers conclude that if your parents were fat, you have more of a chance of growing fat than if your parents were not fat.

I'm waiting for results of the scientific study to determine if the children of parents who conduct a lot of really obvious scientific research are more likely to grow up and conduct a lot of their own really obvious scientific research.

Boston's beleaguered baseball fans spent eighty-six years watching their Red Sox find heartbreaking ways to fall to the "Curse of the Babe" and fail to win the World Series.

Then in 2004 the team finally broke the spell and became world champs. But Boston fans managed to find a downside to coming out on top. As one fan groused, "I'm not sure what we're going to talk about now."

How about the next eighty-six years?

Think your driver's license test was tough? In 2004 the country of Turkmenistan added a new chapter to their test. To get a driver's license, you had to correctly answer questions about the spiritual writings of the nation's president.

There are more people who write poetry than read it. For nearly all of them, poetry doesn't pay.

Then there was the poet Edgar Guest, whose verse so delighted Henry Ford that the automaker gave him a car, making Guest the only person in history to rhyme his way into a free Ford.

Even better was the fortune of an unknown Chicago poet, Harriet Monroe. In 1892 she was commissioned to write an ode for dedication ceremonies at the World's Columbian Exposition in Chicago.

Monroe had no idea what a poet should request for such a commission, so she asked for $1,000. The exposition committee had no idea what to pay for such a poem, so they paid her the $1,000.

This was an extraordinarily large paycheck for a poet. Even today, any poet would be amazed to get paid that much. For Monroe it was only the beginning.

The *New York World* newspaper printed her poem in a story about the exposition but neglected to ask the writer for permission. Monroe sued the paper and won another $5,000.

Total earnings for the poem: $6,000, probably a world record.

Then the tide turned. Harriet Monroe spent several years traveling around Europe on the earnings from that single poem. After returning to Chicago, she rented a hall to give a poetry reading. No one showed up. Everyone had forgotten about her during her years abroad.

When Monroe submitted poems to magazines, they were rejected. When she turned to writing plays, no one would produce them. When she published a book, no one bought it.

But Harriet Monroe would not quit. Observing that nearly all poets were ignored and unpaid, she started a small magazine called *Poetry* in 1911. Hers was the first place of publication, and payment, for many great American poets, including T. S. Eliot, Robert Frost, Vachel Lindsay, Amy Lowell, and Edgar Lee Masters.

The odds that poets will make money from their poetry are actually pretty good. The odds that they will make more than $5 from a lifetime of poetry: not so good. The odds that they will strike it rich? The poets would have a better chance taking their money to Vegas and throwing it all down on Hungry 7 at the roulette wheel.

You know why 7 is the hungry number, don't you? Because 7, 8, 9.

The Russian tsars were leaders in the field of cruel punishments. But they were ahead of the pack in devising unusual punishments too.

1) When someone in his court complained of headaches, Ivan the Terrible ordered his soldiers to drive a nail into the sufferer's head. Didn't cure the headache but did stop the whining.

2) Peter the Great had drunks punished by hanging a seventeen-pound chain around their necks. As if a hangover didn't already feel like a chain around your neck.

Russian premier Nikita Khrushchev took an unbalancing approach to his relations with the statesmen of other nations—alternately charming and threatening them.

He traced this intimidating attitude to the ancient customs of the people of the Caucasus Mountains. "When an enemy is inside your home, sharing your bread and salt, you should always treat him with the greatest hospitality," Khrushchev explained. "But as soon as he steps outside the door, it is all right to slit his throat."

Here's the kind of sports oddity that drives players and fans nuts. The New York Yankees won the World Series five years in a row from 1949 through 1953 without winning 100 games during the regular season.

Then in 1954 the Yanks won 103 games—but didn't even make it into the Series. That was the year the Cleveland Indians became monsters of the American League, taking the title away from New York by winning 111 games.

Then the Indians lost the World Series to the New York Giants without winning a single game.

Alabama fullback Tommy Lewis made one of the most unusual plays in college football history during the 1954 Cotton Bowl. Lewis was standing on the sideline as the running back for Rice

University carried the ball through the Alabama defense for what looked like a sure touchdown.

Before Lewis could stop himself, he ran onto the field and tackled the runner. The stunned referee awarded the stunned Rice team a touchdown, and Rice won the game 28–6.

But that's not the shocker that defied the odds. Lewis went on to coach high school football and didn't talk much about his impulsive move in the Cotton Bowl. So he was astounded when one of his high school players bolted from the bench and made the exact same play during a game, which his school lost by a touchdown.

> ROY SULLIVAN HAD THE KIND OF NICKNAME NO ONE WANTS, BECAUSE YOU HAVE TO EARN IT. A PARK RANGER, SULLIVAN WAS KNOWN AS THE "HUMAN LIGHTNING CONDUCTOR." OVER THIRTY-FIVE YEARS, HE WAS HIT BY LIGHTNING SEVEN TIMES.

In 1997 a baby fell out the window of a seventh-floor apartment in Murcia, Spain, landing on the street below. He defied the odds and lived. If he could have walked, he would have gotten up and walked away from the fall. His only injuries: bruises and a chipped tooth.

Politician Adlai Stevenson ran for president twice but didn't come close to the White House, because he had the misfortune to run against the popular war hero Dwight Eisenhower.

Stevenson took a philosophical view of his plight. "In America any boy may become president," he observed, "and I suppose it's just one of the risks he takes."

Beginnings of enterprises are risky times, when things go wrong that never occurred to you.

Many business ventures don't survive their first year. Some companies that turn out to be giants came perilously close to initial collapse. Consider these off-center beginnings of the giants:

1) In its first year in the soft-drink business, Coca-Cola sold four hundred Cokes.

2) In his first year as a car manufacturer, Henry Ford went bankrupt. Two years later, his second attempt failed. But the third try gave him the top car in America.

3) R. H. Macy went broke with his first three department stores.

4) Paul Galvin failed twice in the storage battery business. The third time, working on borrowed money, he founded Motorola.

5) When King Gillette invented the safety razor in 1903, he sold 51 razors and 168 blades.

6) It took James Watts, a talented repairman, only two days to design the world's first steam engine in 1765. It took him another ten years to produce the first working model.

7) In his first year in the majors, Ty Cobb batted .240. The rookie Reggie Jackson batted .178. They went on to become two of the best hitters of all time.

8) What about the debut films of Hollywood mega-stars? How about these forgettables: Jack Nicholson in *Cry Baby Killer*, Paul Newman in *The Silver Chalice*, Robert Redford in *Warhunt,* and Clint Eastwood in *Francis in the Navy*.

9) As for the great writer O. Henry, in his first year as an author he was sent to prison for embezzlement.

10) In NASA's first twenty-eight attempts to launch rockets, the space agency sent up twenty duds.

11) Czar Ivan was proclaimed emperor of Russia when he was only three months old. He was overthrown before his first birthday.

12) In the Roman Empire's first year, one of the founders killed the other (his brother) in a land dispute.

On the other side of first tries, some tyros shot out of the gate:

1) In their first year as recording artists, the Beatles had four No. 1 songs on the charts.

2) After being rejected by both Hewlett-Packard and Atari, the founders of Apple went into business for themselves and sold $2.5 million of computers in their first year.

3) Jean Paul Getty struck oil with his first oil lease, which he bought for $500 when he was eleven.

If you're already over eleven, you'd better get started.

If you're an actor, the odds against landing a role are bad. They don't necessarily get better even if you're directing the film.

Writer/director John Sayles casts himself in a small role in all his movies. But he wasn't seen on-screen in *Lone Star*, a 1996 drama he wrote, directed, and filmed along the Texas-Mexico border.

"I actually was in a couple of scenes as a Border Patrol guy," Sayles said. "But the scenes were expendable, so I expended myself."

Why did he choose to leave himself on the cutting room floor?

Sayles had a simple explanation: "It was easier for me to cut myself out of a movie than another actor who I talked into coming to rural Texas for less money than he could have made elsewhere."

WRITER HORACE WALPOLE: "NINE-TENTHS OF THE PEOPLE WERE CREATED SO YOU WOULD WANT TO BE WITH THE OTHER TENTH."

"In our brief national history we have shot four of our presidents, worried five of them to death, impeached one, and hounded another out of office," journalist P. J. O'Rourke observed. "And when all else fails, we hold an election and assassinate their character."

A study by Swiss researchers finds that people take revenge on their enemies because it makes them feel good.

Let's see: all over the world, people have been seeking vengeance against each other for thousands of years. And all this time we thought it made them feel worse. It took some researchers from the enlightened country of Switzerland to set us straight.

What are they going to research next: whether conducting inane research makes scientists feel good?

Who's to blame for all the problems of mankind? Men. As in, not women.

Consider education. The fact that you are reading this sentence puts you in a privileged group. Odds are you are not a woman from Egypt, Morocco, Mauritania, or Sudan—countries where more than 50 percent of the women are not taught to read. In Bangladesh, Nepal, Senegal, Benin, and Pakistan, seven out of ten women can't read.

In nearly every country with high illiteracy rates, the rates are much higher for women than for men. Meanwhile, nearly all the major damage done to the world is devised by men who can read.

Boniface VIII held odd views for a pope. What were the odds, he was asked, of the faithful achieving life after death?

About the same as a "roast fowl on the dining table," according to Pope Boniface VIII.

If you suspect you're losing your hair, you're right. It will be little assurance to note that so is everyone else.

Every day everybody loses, on average, fifty hairs from their head. With some people, they grow back.

If you never let anyone cut your hair, it would grow over twenty feet long by the time you lived to seventy-five, if you could live that long without tripping on your hair.

Do parents love their children more now than parents did in the past?

Yes, says Arizona State University's John Corrigan, a professor who studies the history of emotion. "Four hundred years ago, parents wouldn't commit themselves to a deeply loving relationship, because children died younger," he said. "They prepared their children for the hardships of the world by treating them harshly. Now we have a different idea. Our commitment to loving our children is unquestioned."

Why the attitude shift? "You can expect children to live longer," Corrigan said. "Families tend to be smaller, so you don't have to spread around the commitment that comes with love."

As a youngster, the great Russian writer Leo Tolstoy was called Crybaby Leo by his family.

Some kids are crushed by the harsh nicknames they get tagged with. Tolstoy went on to write *War and Peace*.

General George Patton, a fearless American hero in both World Wars, was unafraid to die in battle, because he'd already done it many times, as a reincarnated warrior.

Patton believed he'd been a Greek warrior twice (once serving with Alexander the Great), a Roman bodyguard to Julius Caesar, a knight at the Battle of Crécy, and one of Napoleon's marshals.

If you live to die and die to live again, the fear of death becomes irrelevant.

§EIGHTEEN§

AIMLESS WANDERING AND OTHER OBVIOUS THINGS THAT ARE NOT WHAT THEY APPEAR TO BE

When are beggars not beggars? When they're pretending to be beggars on the path of spiritual enlightenment.

In 2004 a Zen center in England held an unusual retreat, charging students a fee to spend two days on the streets of London pretending to be homeless.

Spiritual retreat activities included begging, hanging around, and aimless wandering. The next time someone asks you to spare a dime, he may actually need that dime—or he may be growing a dime closer to enlightenment.

Very little is actually what it appears to be at first glance, which makes research interesting.

When British designer William Morris visited Paris, he patronized a café at the foot of the Eiffel Tower. A friend commented that Morris must like the tower immensely to show up there every day.

"I remain here," Morris countered, "because it's the only place in Paris where I can avoid seeing the damn thing."

Like sardines? Sorry, there are no sardines, not swimming around the ocean. A sardine is not a fish in the same way that a tuna or a salmon is. A sardine is what the canneries call any small fish stuck in a can. Most popular among sardine canners are the sprat, the pilchard, and the anchoveta—small fish that look remarkably alike when canned.

Menelik II was a forward-thinking emperor of Ethiopia during the early 1900s. When his advisers told him about the new marvel of the western world—the invention of an electric chair to execute criminals—he ordered one for his prison.

The electric chair seemed like a clever way to modernize Ethiopia by increasing the productivity of his kingdom's criminal disposal division. Imagine the emperor's disappointment when the chair arrived and his ministers explained to him that it only worked when powered by electricity, of which Ethiopia at the time had none.

Menelik had the electric chair converted into a royal throne—at which point many of his subjects saw the advantages of modern electricity.

Those neat holes in Swiss cheese? You knew they were bored by bacteria, right? It may be more than you wanted to know that the holes are actually formed by gases emitted by those bacteria. Cheese, and anything else, is rarely as simple as it looks.

If bacterial gases on rye gross you out, buy cheap Swiss cheese. Fast cheese makers skip the traditional aging process and use a drill to bore holes in their cheese. That doesn't improve the taste. They do it so the cheap Swiss looks like the real thing.

When it comes to inaccuracy in reporting the news, TV and radio have seized the initiative from daily newspapers, with the Internet threatening to leapfrog them all.

But back in the 1870s, newspapers had the field of wild inaccuracy to themselves. Thomas Connery, editor of the *New York Herald*, once ran a front-page story about a mass escape of deadly animals from the Central Park Zoo.

According to his report, lions and tigers had raced through Manhattan, killing fifty people. Police and soldiers took to the streets to hunt down those lions the paper said were still on the loose. Panic gripped the city until it was revealed that Connery had made up the entire story.

The ancient Romans didn't believe in throwing criminals in prison. That was the good news. The bad news was they didn't build prisons, because anyone who broke the law or otherwise annoyed the authorities was sent to work in a mine or quarry, where they were sure to die on the job.

The alternative punishment wasn't any better: criminals were sentenced to be the designated victims in the arenas of the gladiators, where they were torn apart by lions, bears, or wolves.

He told the biggest whoppers, outrageous stories about places he couldn't possibly have seen since no one else had. That's why during his lifetime most people didn't believe Marco Polo's stories about exploring China and other exotic lands far from his provincial home in Venice.

The tales of his thirteenth-century travels turned out to be mostly true. They also inspired writers to create their own imaginative fantasies. The adventures of Don Quixote and Baron Munchausen—and the notion that truth can be stranger than fiction—owe much of their flamboyant popularity to the unbelieved but true tales of Marco Polo.

We've all heard of prestigious people who lied about their college degrees and professional credits on their resumes. Looking at the total number of people who apply for jobs in upper and middle management, what percentage of their resumes contain self-aggrandizing lies?

Only 30 percent. We guessed higher.

When Pablo Picasso became a wealthy artist, he bought a classic Hispano-Suiza limousine but not to ride in. He had the car installed inside his studio, where he would meditate in the back seat before beginning a painting.

Connie Chung was working on a TV story during her first trip to Russia. An assistant asked the newscaster if she was having trouble with the Russian language. "Not at all," Chung replied.

"Well," the man said, pointing to a sign in Russian, "then why are you standing in the men's room?"

If you run out of sugar, you run down to the grocery store. People couldn't do that in seventeenth-century Europe. Sugar was sold only at the apothecary shop, because it was considered a medicine. As coffee with sugar became popular, sugar moved over to the grocery shelves.

Speaking of coffee oddities to mull over your morning coffee: In England back in the days before sugar made it from the apothecary to the grocery, people didn't stir sugar into their coffee. They added mustard instead. Don't knock it until you've tried it. Then you can knock it.

To create the great ape's roars for the original *King Kong* movie, sound artists went to the zoo and recorded the roars of lions and tigers at feeding time. Those sounds were played forward and backward simultaneously, and that's how Kong scared kids in the 1930s.

In 1988 officials at McClellan Air Force Base in California explained that civilian mechanics were being "placed on non-duty, non-pay status."

Or as we say in English: They were fired.

Do you know what's in your dinner? A huge swarm of grasshoppers was flying over the mountains of Montana two hundred years ago when they alighted on the snow-covered slopes and froze there by the millions.

Preserved in the ice, the grasshoppers are sometimes defrosted by strong sunshine and become dinner for the birds of Montana, who have no idea they're dining on two-hundred-year-old grasshoppers. Anyone know if an old frozen grasshopper tastes about the same as a fresh one?

Marie Antoinette was the fashion trendsetter in eighteenth-century France. Women of style imitated the queen's every look.

When Marie became pregnant, the fashionable ladies of Paris took to wearing pillows under their dresses in stylish imitation of the queen's new look. As Marie's pregnancy grew, so did the plump of the ladies' pillows. Once the royal baby was born, the pillow look went out of style.

Marie Antoinette set fashion trends even when she was too dead to appreciate her influence in society. After Marie was beheaded during the Reign of Terror, young women in England and France copied the queen's guillotine fashion. They cut their hair short and sported red ribbons tied around their necks at the cut line.

In 1904 a woman was arrested in New York City for performing an indecent act in public.

Her crime? Smoking a cigarette.

Most writers would never admit to what British writer A. N. Wilson owned up to: "If you know somebody is going to be awfully annoyed by something you write, that's obviously very satisfying. And if they howl with rage or cry, that's honey."

When Franz Liszt became popular throughout Europe, fans of his music beseeched him for locks of his hair. The demand for Lisztean hair grew so great that the composer began cutting hair from his dog and sending that to his fans.

In attics throughout Europe, pressed between the pages of diaries as family heirlooms, are locks of hair from the great composer or, in some cases, from the composer's dog. The collectors will never know which.

Among the famous, even their names aren't what they appear to be.

1) Movie star Gary Cooper had a minor name change. He was actually Frank Cooper, but his agent didn't like the sound of Frank. She changed his name to honor her hometown: Gary, Indiana.

Coop's reaction? "It's a good thing she didn't come from Poughkeepsie."

2) The great pianist Vladimir Horowitz was as eccentric in his daily life as he was virtuosic on the keyboard. And it all began with the smallest of name changes.

When Vladimir left Russia in 1925 to become a professional pianist in Germany, he changed his last name but only by one letter—from Gorowitz to Horowitz.

3) People name their kids for all kinds of odd reasons, but basically because the baby's too young to argue. Belle Starr, the Bandit Queen of the Wild West, named daughter Pearl after her favorite gun—a pearl-handled revolver given to her by the child's father, the outlaw Cole Younger, who got a teenage Belle pregnant, then sent her home.

Pearl, like her mother, grew up running from the law and ducking bullets. Later in life, she ran a brothel.

In the early 1800s a French girl, Amantine-Aurore-Lucile Dupin, changed her name to George Sand and went on to become famous as a woman writing under a man's name.

It was her father's idea to dress her as a boy, so she could accompany him places that girls didn't go in stuffy French society.

When she grew up, Sand enjoyed male society and a good cigar. She continued to dress in men's clothing and took bohemian poets, musicians, and artists as her lovers.

Most of us wear them; some of us collect them. But few of us think about shoes like writer Nicholson Baker, who noted that shoes are "the first adult machines we are given to master."

Supreme Court judges are chosen with sober deliberation. Lawyers must pass tough bar exams. Juries are selected only after much maneuvering.

Then it takes someone like the anti-establishment writer Charles Bukowski to explode the entire pretense.

"Courts are places where the ending is written first," Bukowski said, "and all that precedes is simply vaudeville."

History is being made every day all around us but not always in the most obvious ways, according to Wild West historian Bob Boze Bell.

"Billy the Kid was a busboy at a hotel in Arizona," he said. "If you had asked the generals and senators who ate there, 'Who is going to be the one person remembered from your time?' none of them would have said, 'That busboy back in the kitchen.'

"It's endlessly fascinating to me who will be remembered from our time, and I don't think it will be who we think it will be."

A provocative extension of that notion comes from former U.S. Attorney General Ramsey Clark, who pointed out: "If Rosa Parks had not refused to move to the back of the bus, you and I might never have heard of Dr. Martin Luther King."

Movie fights may be faked, but that doesn't mean they're not dangerous, especially if you're not the star.

Actor Everett McGill played the villain in the Steven Seagal action film *Under Siege 2: Dark Territory*. In the big fight scene, McGill found himself on the receiving end of Seagal's biggest punches—and they weren't faked.

"Seagal has one thing to offer," McGill said, "the truth of what he does as a fighter. For him to pull punches in a fight, he can't sell it."

Seagal and McGill worked out a system for the star to hit his co-star. "We came to an arrangement that I would take the body blows," McGill said.

The system didn't work the other way around. McGill pulled his punches. It had nothing to do with egos. "If you lost a major actor because of a broken jaw, the project collapses," McGill explained.

When making the low-budget comedy *Swingers*, movie director Doug Liman didn't have enough money to re-create an LA nightclub. So he took his cast into a popular bar on a crowded night and shot the scene in a real setting.

Liman was technically able to shoot in a real club, instead of a movie set, because he used a small camera, about the size of a shoebox, and a film stock that didn't require Hollywood lighting.

Some people in the bar knew Liman was filming for a movie. Some didn't. "In LA it would be uncool for people to ask if you're making a movie," Liman said. "There's so much attitude in Hollywood, and that's exactly what we were trying to capture."

Liman ran into an unexpected problem while shooting the bar scene that actually improved the film. When Mike (played by Jon Favreau) tried to pick up the beautiful Lorraine (Heather Graham), he found another guy already hitting on her. "This guy had no idea we were in the middle of a movie," the director recalled. "So Jon cuts in, and you can see the guy glaring at him for the rest of the scene.

"The guy must have thought he was witnessing the ultimate pickup because Heather was so responsive to Jon."

So, guys, the next time you're trying to interest a beautiful woman, make sure to bring a film crew with you.

In the fifth century while baptizing King Aengus, Saint Patrick accidentally leaned on his pointed staff, stabbing the king's foot. After the ceremony, Patrick realized the king's foot was bleeding badly and apologized for his clumsiness. "Why did you suffer this pain in silence?" he asked.

The king shrugged and said, "I thought it was part of the ritual."

Does the writer and artist Maurice Sendak write books for kids? Yes and no. Take his classic *Where the Wild Things Are*. Sort of a kids' book but full of edgy ideas.

Sendak even had two ways of talking about the book. When children asked him what happened to the wild hero Max after the book ended, Sendak would tell them "upbeat stories, like he's an astronaut now or a pilot."

But if an adult asked the same question, Sendak would shake his head and reply, "Max is still in therapy and lives with his mother."

Movie stars have a great life, except for the odd pitfalls of fan gush. Take what happened to George Clooney when the Hollywood star ran into a guy from his hometown of Cincinnati, who reminisced: "I grew up watching your brother Nick on TV."

"That wasn't my brother," Clooney told the fan. "That was my father. So I guess I'm getting older."

A small businessman saw a way to turn a quick buck during Pope John Paul II's visit to Miami in 1987. He printed up commemorative T-shirts in Spanish to sell to Miami's large Spanish-speaking population.

The T-shirt man made one little mistake, because he didn't speak Spanish as well as the people who ended up laughing over his shirts. He wanted to sell them a shirt that said, "I saw the pope (el papa)." And he came close, calling John Paul "la papa." In English that would be: "I saw the potato."

Baltimore Orioles manager Earl Weaver: "Smart managing is dumb. The three-run homer you trade for in the winter will always beat brains."

WRITER KIN HUBBARD: "I'LL BET THE HARDEST THING ABOUT PRIZEFIGHTING IS PICKING UP YOUR TEETH WITH A BOXING GLOVE ON."

Comic Emo Philips: "I'm walking home from school, watching some men building a new house. And the guy hammering on the roof calls me a paranoid little weirdo. In Morse code."

❧ NINETEEN ❧

A LEVEL 5 WORLD:
HOW THEY'RE MAKING OUR
FUTURE EVEN STRANGER

British scientists predict that as England's rivers get more polluted, more male fish will turn into female fish. I suppose the good news here is that it eliminates competition for the fish that remain male.

But the weird way things are going, the future will be even stranger than the experts predict.

Try this one on your mom, kids. When she orders, "Clean your room," explain to her the different meanings of the concept "clean," and that you're prepared to adopt the standards of Western Michigan University.

In 2004 that institute of higher learning ran into budget problems, which all of its higher education somehow didn't make it smart enough to handle. Instead, the university's custodial department led the way into a future of lowered expectations by redefining what they meant by "clean."

Not having the janitorial power to keep the classrooms and other facilities clean by the standards of what people thought they meant by clean, they simply switched to a "Level 5" clean.

Level 5 called for dirty or scuffed floors; walls with gum, stains, dirt, and dust balls; light fixtures that were "dirty with dust balls and flies;" "trash containers and pencil sharpeners overflow;" and "trash containers smell sour."

Kids everywhere would be happy to negotiate with mom to keep their rooms university-clean. But the WMU vision goes far beyond janitorial services. They're pointing the way to a future when all negatives that can't be dealt with are simply "repositivized."

Consider government. Since there aren't many wars left that we can win and have them stay won, we'll simply change the standards of military engagement to a Level 5 victory: invaded country successfully left in utter chaos with ruins everywhere. Countryside will be overrun with insurgents, flies, and dust balls. Cities overflow with trash and bombs. Superlative job, men.

Or take a look at the high school of the future. Since we can't actually teach your kids much, the schools will simply graduate them with a Level 5 education: upon graduation, students will be able to spell "dust balls." Their minds will overflow with trash, and they will smell sour, but pencil sharpeners are likely to be clean.

O r the future might look more "Ballardized."

"I would sum up my fear about the future in one word: boring," writer J. G. Ballard said. "Nothing exciting or new or interesting is ever going to happen again. The future is just going to be a vast, conforming suburb of the soul."

T he next time an apocalyptic visionary tells you the world is going to end on Thursday, be sure to ask which Thursday.

Predicting the immediate end of the world "has been going on since the time of Alexander the Great," according to Pat Dickerson, a professor of religious history at Arizona State University. "All the early New Testament writers thought the world was going to end immediately."

They weren't alone. There have been innumerable prophets predicting the end of the world. Robert Reidt was one of the few who had a good explanation as to what *ruined* the end of the world.

At midnight on February 13, 1925, Reidt and his followers gathered in their white robes, waiting for the angel Gabriel to raise them up to heaven.

Didn't happen, and Reidt knew who to blame for the world not coming to the predicted end. It was the fault of the newspaper photographers who had come to take their picture as the Reidtites rose up through the sky. Reidt accused the photogs of ruining the end of the world "with the flashbulbs from your cameras."

Doom-saying isn't the exclusive province of religious world-enders. It's a predictive game that you can play without any training or qualifications. All you need is someone to believe you. These people all found numerous followers ready to give it up:

German professor Johannes Stoeffler predicted the world would end by flood on February 20, 1524.

English mathematician William Whiston agreed with the flood scenario but changed the end date to October 13, 1736.

The flooding theory gained popularity once more when an English soldier named William Bell convinced people that doomsday would drown everyone on April 5, 1761.

William Miller, a farmer turned preacher, gave his followers one year—between March 21, 1843, and March 21, 1844—to prepare themselves, because Jesus was coming and would "bring all his saints with him."

When Christ failed to materialize, the Millerites shifted the end of the world to October 22, 1844. On that day, Miller's followers gathered to await the end together. Later, they all went home.

In 1903 historian Henry Adams calculated 1950 as "the year when the world must go smash."

In 1925 Margaret Rowen, head of the Church of Advanced Adventists, announced February 6 or 7 of that year, "shortly after midnight," as the time when Jesus would "meet his 144,000 faithful."

In 1910 Charles Russell, who founded the Jehovah's Witnesses, said, "The deliverance of the saints must take place sometime before 1914." When 1914 passed, Russell simply extended his prediction that the saints would be delivered "sometime after 1914."

Numerous prophets predicted the end of the world in the year 1998, because Jesus had been crucified in the 1,998th week of his life.

A psychic named Criswell said the Earth would lose all its oxygen and crash into the sun in 1999.

Professor Dickerson explained why the inaccuracy of these prophecies never bothers the people who buy into the next doomsday prophecy.

"When the prophecies are disconfirmed because the world doesn't end, they are just absorbed into the next layer," Dickerson said. "You always punt into the future. There's always a new generation that doesn't understand that people have done this all before. Everybody comes in at the first generation."

Unless, of course, we're now at the last generation. If so, you read it here first.

Predictors of doom have had more success on a personal level.
1) In 1977 rock band Lynyrd Skynyrd put out an album called *Street*

Survivor, whose cover depicted the band in flames. A week later the band's plane crashed in Mississippi and two members died, including lead singer Ronnie Van Zant.

Half a million copies of the album had already been sold. The rest were recalled, and a new flameless picture of the band was substituted.

The hit single on the album? "That Smell," whose chorus ran, "Ooh, ooh, that smell. The smell of death's around you."

2) The popular Glenn Miller and his army band were entertaining troops during World War II. Stationed in London, Miller decided to fly ahead of the band for a show in Paris, which had just been liberated from the Germans.

Before he took off, Miller told the band, "I have an awful feeling you guys are going to go home without me, and I'm going to get mine in some goddamn beat-up old plane." Miller's plane disappeared over the English Channel.

3) Margaret Mitchell, who wrote the novel *Gone with the Wind,* was killed crossing the street, hit by a speeding car. After she died, one of her friends recalled a letter Mitchell had sent him in which she wrote, "I'm going to die in a car crash. I feel very certain of this."

If one final trip is in your future, you might want to plan a little more thoroughly, as the Egyptians once did.

When mummies were buried in the tombs of ancient Egypt, they were provided with supplies for their life in the next world—including maps showing them how to get there.

In 2004 the U.S. military had seventeen brigades stationed in Iraq, fighting a war that had grown tougher once victory had been declared. Pentagon strategists may have been at a loss as to how to defeat the insurgents, but they were not at a loss when it came to verbal smokescreens.

When asked how the military would respond if forced to fight another war at the same time, government officials explained that America would simply win the second war "less quickly."

That's reassuring. And it opens a future line of excuse-making for other government officials.

The next time we have a major disaster and the rescue squad screws up the relief effort, they can say, "We didn't lose nearly as many potential survivors as we could have lost if we had screwed up worse."

Or the president could explain that it only appears like he's doing nothing to help the poor, while actually he's making them rich less quickly (and, therefore, eligible for plenty of government assistance).

Many people think that in the future they'll be eating Twinkies made long ago. They think Twinkies last on store shelves for years, decades, forever. That notion comes straight from the Snack Department of the School of Urban Myths.

Twinkies sell so rapidly and are consumed so quickly that they don't have time to sit on store shelves. Americans eat five hundred million Twinkies a year.

> EACH YEAR YOU WAIT TO CLIMB MOUNT EVEREST, IT GETS A LITTLE TOUGHER TO DO. THAT'S BECAUSE THE HIMALAYAS GROW HALF AN INCH A YEAR.

People will tell you, "You can't live in the past." Oddly enough, you can't help living in the past. We all do it, all the time.

Without light, no life. With light, the past is always upon us. Sunlight is always eight-minute-old sunlight, because that's how long it takes light to reach the Earth.

Starlight? You don't see stars at night. You see what the stars used to be, like a portrait of a person long dead.

Let's say the light from a star takes twenty million years to reach us. As we're gazing at that star, it may have exploded and disappeared ten million years ago, and we won't even know it for another ten million years. Stay tuned.

As television became the dominant commonality, German psychologists studied the effects of TV withdrawal on people who watched a lot of television. In a 1971 experiment, they paid people to shut off their TV sets and leave them off. No TV at all.

Most of the test subjects gave up the money and went back to watching TV after a few days. No one in the study lasted more than five months without television. And the scientists found a creepy side effect of TV withdrawal—an increase in child abuse.

Here's something to look forward to in those odd moments when the future looks safe: "If the Third World War is fought with nuclear weapons," British naval commander Louis Mountbatten said, "the fourth will be fought with bows and arrows."

"If an alien race came here to explore the dominant life form on this planet, they wouldn't be up here with us," said Bruce Robison, a biologist who spent twenty-five years studying animals of the deep. "They would be down in the ocean."

Two of the weird deep-sea marvels Robison studied: the gulper eel and the jelly web.

Food is scarce far below, and the hunters of the deep have adapted. The gulper eel's mouth and stomach are so large and elastic that the eel can swallow fish bigger than itself.

Many people are, judging by their expansion modes, trying to master that trick. But they can't do it all in one gulp.

The jelly web deep in the ocean is composed of cooperative colonies of gelatinous creatures called siphonophores. These miniature jellies are less than an inch in length, yet they link to form functioning chains up to 120 feet long. They work together better than the Steelers' front line.

If ocean life doesn't dominate, then the future may belong to the insects. They outweigh us. Total up all the insects on the planet, then all the people — and the insects would tip the scales, ten times as heavy as we are.

Or look at it this way: all the people and other animals represent 15 percent of animal life on Earth. The insects comprise the other 85 percent.

TWENTY

THE ONE-DAY PRESIDENT
AND OTHER ODDS AND ENDS

Most of us have wondered at one time or another: What's the difference between a beauty contest and a dog show?

Los Angeles TV personality Bill Weir can explain, because he covered both events. At the dog show, he had to step around dog droppings on the arena floor. "You almost never see this type of thing in the Miss America competition," Weir commented.

In my book, there's nothing odder than odds and ends.

In 1974 someone put two loads into a freighter headed for Wales: lumber and tapioca. As the ship came into the port of Cardiff, a fire started in the lumber hold. The shore patrol pumped water into the ship to put out the flames. The water activated the tapioca powder, which was heated by the fire.

Suddenly, the cry went up: "Ahoy, pudding!"

The ship's hold was filled with a few million gallons of tapioca. It took a fleet of dump trucks to relieve the ship of its bizarre burden.

Olympic moments of the non-TV kind:

1) We've all had this dream, haven't we? You're swimming in a pool filled with spaghetti, your feet covered with thick honey.

   Australian swimmer Dawn Fraser had that dream in 1956 on the night before she was to swim in the finals of the Olympic 100-meter freestyle. Fraser was such a great swimmer that the next day she overcame her nightmare and all the other swimmers to win the gold medal.

2) In 1972 before he went for the gold in weightlifting's heavyweight division, the Russian hopeful Vassily Alexeyev ate a heavyweight breakfast: twenty-six fried eggs, the monotony of which he broke with a steak. Then he went out and lifted the gold.

3) To keep her nerves under control in the 1984 Olympics, Canadian diver Sylvie Bernier drowned out the poolside announcer by listening to the soundtrack from *Flashdance* in her head-

phones over and over again before each dive. Won a gold medal that way.

4) Cuban runner Felix Carvajal wanted to compete in the 1904 Olympics in St. Louis. But the Cuban government wouldn't support him. So Carvajal paid his own way to the United States.

He stopped off in New Orleans and got into a craps game. The hustlers took him for all the money he had. Carvajal hitched a ride to St. Louis, arriving only minutes before his race was to start. He was still in his long pants and wore his traveling boots. No Nikes back then.

Olympic officials held up the start of the race while Carvajal cut his pants into shorts. He then ran in his boots.

But he didn't win. He came in that toughest of all Olympic positions: fourth place.

Odd Olympic nicknames: gymnast Olga Korbut, the Munchkin of Munich; swimmer Murray Rose (who was a vegetarian), the Seaweed Streak; swimmer Arne Borg (who wasn't a fish), the Swedish Sturgeon; and gymnast Pete DesJardins, the Little Bronze Statue from Florida.

Y ou probably knew that the last time we had a month without a
full moon was February 1866. When will this phenomenon
happen again?

In two million years. Don't know about you, but I can't wait.

W hen offended gentlemen of the eighteenth century challenged
their rivals to a duel, why was dawn the preferred time for a
civilized shootout?

It was preferable to get gut-shot before breakfast, because you
had a better chance of surviving on an empty stomach than a full one.

A mong White House oddities, we have the president who
shouldn't have been, the president who was but no one remembers him, and the president who thought he was but wasn't:

1) Samuel Tilden came closer to the presidency than Al Gore. In
1876 Tilden, the governor of New York, appeared to have won a
close presidential election.

There was confusion in Washington (now that's a surprise)
with four states submitting double sets of voting results, and
other states reporting that voters had been forced out of the
polling places.

A congressional committee investigated the mess and
resolved it with a back-room deal. That's how Rutherford B.

Hayes was declared president with a 185-184 edge in the Electoral College. Tilden had won the popular vote by 250,000.

2) More legitimate, though shorter termed and less remembered, was David Atchison, the eleventh-and-a-half president of the United States.

Happened this way: James Polk, our eleventh president, left office on March 4, 1849, when No. 12, Zachary Taylor, was scheduled to assume the presidency.

But as calendar fans know, March 4 of that year fell on a Sunday. The devoutly religious Taylor could not violate the Sabbath and take the oath of office on a Sunday.

Missouri Senator David Atchison, next in the line of succession as president pro tempore of the Senate, took over the White House for a single day, from noon Sunday to noon Monday.

What did Atchison do during his term in office? Appointed some friends to cabinet positions, had a drink, and went to bed. In other words, he accomplished as much and did less harm than other politicians who filled the office for four years instead of one day.

3) Al Gore and George W. Bush weren't the first candidates to get confused over who was headed to the White House on election night.

As the big night wore on back in 1916, it became obvious to everyone that the Democratic candidate Woodrow Wilson was going to lose. As state tallies rolled slowly in, the Republicans became so confident of victory that their man, Charles Evans Hughes, went to bed early, dreaming of his White House years.

During the long night, Wilson crept closer, then passed Hughes, and won the election by twenty-three electoral votes.

The first reporter who rushed up to Hughes's hotel suite to get his reaction to the bad news was blocked by an ill-informed Republican functionary, who told the reporter, "The president is sleeping and must not be disturbed," but the reporter could leave a message.

"Tell the president," the reporter snapped, "that he ain't president."

More presidential oddities:

1) When Andrew Johnson was in the White House, he kept pet mice in the basement, feeding them on flour and water.

2) When Richard Nixon left the White House in disgrace, a French company marketed an audiotape of his resignation speech. The speech wasn't long enough to fill the tape, so the manufacturers finished it off with poetry. Whose? The odes of John Keats.

3) Calvin Coolidge slept ten hours a night. Were those more innocent times? Or was the country better off with a president who was unconscious nearly half the day?

Presidents have a knack for stating the obvious as if it had just occurred to them, which perhaps it had. Here are a few presidents who entertained the White House press corps.

1) President Lyndon Johnson: "For the first time in history, profits are higher than ever before."

2) President Dwight Eisenhower: "Things have never been more like they are today in history."

3) President Calvin Coolidge: "When more and more people are thrown out of work, unemployment results."

4) President George H. W. Bush: "I have opinions of my own, strong opinions, but I don't always agree with them."

The twentieth century was marked by two of history's biggest wars. Under their shadow, we forget the century's longest and shortest wars.

Andorra, the tiny Pyrenees mountain republic located between Spain and France, joined the allies in the fight against Germany during World War I. When the peace conference was convened in Versailles, the world's powers forgot to invite Andorra.

Before the government of Andorra could arrange a peace with Germany, World War II came around, so Andorra simply continued in its state of war. Peace between Andorra and Germany was finally declared in 1958 when someone noticed that no one had settled a war that hadn't been fought for over a decade.

As for the century's shortest war, which is usually the best kind: when El Salvador's soccer squad beat the Honduras team 3-0 in the qualifying round for the 1970 World Cup, the two nations went to war. After soldiers fired at each other across the border for half an hour, the two sides declared peace.

In 1891 a harpooner on a British whaling ship fell into the ocean and was swallowed whole by a sperm whale. The ship pursued the whale, and the sailors managed to kill it after several hours. When the whale was cut open, the harpooner was found in its stomach and alive.

The sailor recovered from the ordeal, but his hair and skin had been bleached white by fluids in the whale's stomach.

In October of 2001 when people around the United States were flying the flag, an antique shop in Santa Cruz, California, put an odd arrangement in its display window: a dozen small American flags surrounding a group of apples arranged to spell out: "USA."

Good to live in a country where even the fruit is patriotic.

In showbiz there are stars and flops. Then there are stars who become flops who become stars.
1) For years Oscar Hammerstein II and Jerome Kern were a hot

Broadway songwriting duo. After they broke up, Hammerstein had nothing but flops for ten years. Then he teamed up with Richard Rodgers, and the two of them wrote one of the biggest Broadway musicals of all time: *Oklahoma!*

2) Burt Bacharach was a big success early in his songwriting career. Then he fell off the charts for a decade. When he returned with the theme song for the movie *Arthur*, he not only had a hit, he won an Oscar for Best Song.

3) Kenny Rogers rode the pogo stick of fame. He first made it big with the New Christy Minstrels. When that group faded, Rogers revived his career with the First Edition. They had a big hit with *Ruby, Don't Take Your Love to Town*, a song written ten years before it was recorded.

After the First Edition broke up, Rogers dropped out again. A decade later, he came back for a third time, as a solo act bigger than either of his first two incarnations.

It's a crazy world, but hey, that's showbiz.

During the Revolutionary War, about five thousand slaves fought on the side of the American insurrectionists, helping the new nation win its independence even though they were denied their own.

Many of these black soldiers were sent by white slave owners to fight in their place. The slaves took the risks, while the masters took the soldiers' pay.

By the time the United States entered World War I, conditions in the army had changed but not enough. A division of black American soldiers was sent to fight in France but was denied the right to wear the uniforms of their country, at the insistence of racist white officers.

Instead, the American soldiers were given French uniforms. The French army was so desperate at that point in the war against Germany, they took anyone with a gun.

Horses were used to pull carts and drag loads for centuries before the horse collar was invented in the second century. How was the cart attached to the horse? To their tails.

ANCIENT EGYPTIANS THOUGHT THEIR PET CATS LOOKED ESPECIALLY GOOD WEARING EARRINGS. HISTORIANS DON'T NOTE WHAT THE CATS THOUGHT OF THE STYLE.

Did you eat four and a half pounds of licorice last year? If you live in Holland, you probably did. That's the national average for the Dutch, major consumers of licorice since the thirteenth century.

No one goes to Vegas casinos for their health. That didn't stop one Nevada casino from introducing the Pedal 'n' Play—a slot machine activated by an exercise bicycle. That way aerobic gamblers could burn away their calories and their money at the same time.

Shakespearean students like to play around with this one: in the forty-sixth Psalm of the King James Bible, the forty-sixth word from the start is "shake," and the forty-sixth word from the end is "spear."

Now look at the Bard's name, using one of the old spellings: Shakspeare. Break it into two syllables and you get one syllable with four letters and one with six.

When director Rusty Cundieff made the horror film *Tales from the Hood*, it reminded him of how scared he was as a kid when he saw *The Exorcist*. "It had me shook up for weeks," he said. "I was afraid to go to bed. I rationalized that the devil might be able to lift up a bed, but he wouldn't be strong enough to lift a bunk bed."

As an adult, horror movies no longer scare him. "What really scares me are not monsters but a lot of the people I meet on a day-to-day basis," he said. "I'm more concerned with stopping at a cash machine at night then I am walking through a cemetery. Dead people, in general, don't bother you."

Before Lauritz Melchior became a world-famous tenor, he was a starving music student in Munich. One day while practicing an opera in the garden, he sang, "Come to me, my love, on the wings of light."

Melchior heard a strange sound from above. He looked up as a beautiful woman in white fell from the sky and landed at his feet.

Then he saw the parachute. She wasn't an angel but the Bavarian actress Maria Hacker. She had been performing a skydiving stunt for a movie production and had gotten blown off course when her chute opened.

"I thought that she came to me from heaven," Melchior recalled years later. "I still think so."

Five odd thoughts to end the odds and ends with:

1) Comic Victor Borge: "Did you know Mozart had no arms and no legs? I've seen statues of him on people's pianos."

2) Writer George Bernard Shaw: "Why should we take advice on sex from the pope? If he knows anything about it, he shouldn't."

3) Comic George Carlin: "What do you do when you see an endangered animal eating an endangered plant?"

4) Comic Bobby Kelton: "Why is a birthday cake the only food you can blow on and spit on and everybody rushes to get a piece?"

5) Cartoonist Charles Schulz: "My life has no purpose, no direction, no aim, no meaning, and yet I'm happy. I can't figure it out. What am I doing right?"

PART 2

TWENTY-ONE

DIFFERENT LIVES

Some people defy the odds and do what the rest of us never will. They take us along on their unique journeys through the stories they bring back.

THE LONER
Your world changes completely when you move at a different pace. Take Jeff Clifford of Arizona, who crept through the jungle at two hundred yards an hour as a Marine sniper in the Vietnam War.

When Clifford went to Fort Pendleton's Scout-Sniper School, he was trained to shoot people at eleven hundred yards. Picture ten football fields lined up end to end. Your target is in the far end zone of the tenth field, visible only through a high-powered scope.

Marine snipers perfect their technique by firing one thousand rounds a day, "until your shoulder becomes black and blue, and then toughens so you don't flinch when you shoot," Clifford said.

"You trained hard enough that you never missed."

Snipers also train to survive in enemy territory without any support. They stay alive only as long as they remain undetectable. They move in on their targets at incredibly slow speeds, so no one can spot the motion.

"It once took me five hours to crawl a thousand yards to set up a target," Clifford said. "You crawl to look like the rustling of the wind on bushes. I once had an enemy soldier standing five feet from me, and he couldn't see me."

Snipers even have a different sense of being unconscious. "We were taught to put ourselves to sleep but always be on alert status," Clifford said. "I used to sleep by tying myself to the roots of a tree at the edge of a cliff because no one else would walk on the cliff at night."

Then there's the different sense of mortality they develop. New snipers who find they can't pull the trigger on a live target are reassigned. They may be the lucky ones.

After serving two years with a sniper unit in Vietnam, Clifford said there were only "four of us left alive, and all of us had been wounded by counter-snipers or enemy patrols who hunted us down. That's why it's all volunteer work."

THE SURVIVORS

We call them heroes because we need to. But they understand the shifting truths of extreme situations in ways someone who hasn't been through their ordeal never can.

In 1972 a plane chartered by a rugby team from Uruguay crashed high in the Andes Mountains and broke in two. Those young men who survived the crash were stranded in the snow and ice for seventy days without food or adequate clothing. They were given up for dead by the search teams. Yet sixteen of the forty-five passengers survived the ordeal.

"People see us as heroes," one of the survivors, Robert Canessa, said twenty years later. "But while it was going on, I never felt more horrible in my life. Now that I'm just normal, I feel good. But when I was a hero, I felt horrible.

"I envied the ones who were dead. Our broken plane, which had been a hotel, was now a coffin."

For two months the men huddled together against freezing winds inside the busted shell of the plane. Without food, they decided to eat meat from their dead and frozen friends.

"We thought about God," Carlitos Paez said, "that Jesus gave his body to save humanity, and our friends sacrificed their bodies to save their friends."

One night, the plane was buried under an avalanche and more of them died, suffocated by the snow. "I gave up under the snow," Canessa said. "I thought, what's the point of having the agony if we are not going to survive? But someone took the snow off my face, so I went on."

In the middle of a snowstorm, Canessa and another survivor, Nando Parrado, decided they would rather die walking off the mountain. They knew if they left their broken shelter, they would freeze to death at night or fall to their death off a cliff in the storm.

They walked for days, searching for a way down out of the snowfields into the green valleys of Chile. "I don't know how we survived that walk," Canessa said. "I thought all the time that we would freeze to death. But the next hour we were still alive, so we kept going."

Twelve days later, they made it off the ice and found help for their friends on the mountain. The terrible irony? Two days after the crash, a search plane had passed directly over them and didn't see them partially buried in the snow.

When the world learned how the men had survived without food, some people reacted with repulsion. Others understood the choice they had made. The survivors received a telegram from the pope, who acknowledged that "we did what we must do," Paez said.

"People in our country felt we were *their* survivors," Canessa added. "We belonged to the people's feelings. I have learned your life can change immediately. You learn not to hesitate in your life, to go in and do your best."

"If you could go through the mountains, living the rest of your life is quite easy," Paez said.

DOCTOR OF GIANTS

One unusual side effect of a life behind bars: the animals in a zoo live far longer than they would in the wild. Some live so long, they end up dying of cancer or heart problems that are rare in their natural habitats.

Herbivores like ibex and goats may grow so old in the security of a zoo that they wear down their teeth and can no longer chew their food.

Before zookeepers stopped the practice, goats and sheep in children's petting zoos died from being overfed by friendly kids. The animals grew too fat—like many of the kids themselves—and developed arteriosclerosis.

Other zoo animals fell victim to vandals who snuck in after hours to torment them.

In the Phoenix Zoo, an emu died from eating a piece of glass someone threw into the cage. Another person taunted a bobcat by flapping a glove against the bars. The bobcat was quicker than the person expected. It reached through the bars, snagged the glove, and ate it.

But the zoo surgeon, Dr. Kathy Orr, opened the bobcat's stomach, pulled out the remnants of the glove, and saved the animal's life.

Orr could do nothing to save a rhea that got stuck in the mud and broke a leg after vandals broke into the zoo at night to chase the birds around.

Some zoo animals die from too much civilization. At the Phoenix Zoo, a zebra, spooked by planes flying overhead, charged into a fence and broke its neck.

Among all the animals, giraffes are the trickiest to help medically, because they are so tall and thin. "They injure themselves just in the act of lying down," Dr. Orr said.

Operating on a giraffe is difficult because of its powerful heart, which must be strong enough to pump blood all the way up that incredibly long neck to the giraffe's head.

When a giraffe lies down, the heart pumps too strongly, raising the animal's blood pressure to dangerous levels. When Dr. Orr operates on a giraffe, she rests the animal's head on a stack of hay bales to keep it elevated and the blood pressure down.

Warning: If you don't like the gross stuff, skip to the next story now.

Bet you're still with me. Time to talk about what they do with zoo animals when they die behind bars. They bury them, mostly, typically in a spot in the zoo shielded from the public view. Some zoos incinerate their dead.

Either way, think about elephants. Too big for the furnace, too big to bury. Before the elephants, rhinos, giraffes, and other zoo giants can be buried, they must be chainsawed into pieces.

"It's just as much work to get them small enough to fit in the incinerator as it is to bury them," Dr. Orr said. "Burying them seems more environmentally correct because of air quality regulations."

Not all animal parts are buried. Some skulls and bones will be used for education purposes in zoo programs or college classes. These parts are first sent to university biology departments, where beetle colonies clean them to the bone.

Hope you've enjoyed your tour of the hidden zoo you don't see on a Saturday morning walk-around.

THE HERO

"I don't know anyone in the Society of the Medal of Honor who believes they deserve the medal," said Fred Ferguson, a pilot instructor for the Arizona Army National Guard. "I know I don't. If you look at what the other guys did, you think: That's better than what I did."

Ferguson won the military's highest tribute in 1968 during the Vietnam War. He flew his helicopter through heavy mortar and rifle fire to rescue the crew and passengers of another chopper that had been shot down behind enemy lines.

"We did not have to attempt a rescue," Ferguson recalled. "Three other copters had tried rescues but been driven off by heavy fire.

"One of the prerequisites of the medal is that if you didn't do it, no one would think the less of you. If it's your job and you're supposed to do it, they don't give you a medal for it. That's what you get paid for."

Ferguson flew in and got the others out alive. "It was pure dumb luck that we pulled it off," he said. "There was skill and planning and professionalism but also dumb luck.

"Things can turn bad really quickly, and sometimes there's no rhyme nor reason for it. In battle you sit and you sit and you wait, and all of a sudden you're up to your ass in alligators. This goes on for a few minutes, and then you sit there again. Hours of boredom spelled by stark terror."

Years later, Ferguson can recall the rescue in detail. "We were so intent on getting done what we needed done that we ignored the heavy fire and never thought of turning back," he remembered. "Failure was not something we thought about. We were getting shot up, but so what?"

And that's the attitude that occasionally leads soldiers to win the Medal of Honor.

THE DOOMED

"Nevermore!"

If any writer owns a word in the English language, it's Edgar Allan Poe, poet of doom. His quotable raven gave that word a resonant gloom that's unshakable.

"Nevermore." Lost for eternity. But also lost moment by moment. Nothing holds. Nothing to hold onto.

How did such a talented writer develop such a morbid world view? We need look no further than the pit and pendulum that was his life, a tale of woe as perverse as Poe's fantasies.

When Poe was an infant, his father deserted the family. His mother starved to death, leaving three children penniless. His retarded sister lived out her misery in an asylum. His older brother was killed in a brawl.

Provided an education by a wealthy couple, who took him in out of pity but refused to adopt him, Poe became a drunk at the age of eleven.

Blessed and cursed with intelligence, Poe could not contain his self-destructive impulses long enough to finish a university education. Then he was drummed out of West Point. He turned to writing to support his alcohol and drug habits.

Although many of his poems and stories were published, he was not recognized as a great writer during his life and was paid little for his work. Poe received $10 for his greatest poem, "The Raven," which has since been published in countless volumes, none of which had to pay him, since he drank himself to death at the age of forty.

Edgar Allan Poe walked alone through a life of madness and morbidity. But the path of self-destruction is wide enough for all the artists and writers who use alcohol and drugs to summon their talents.

"All art is a kind of subconscious madness expressed in terms of sanity," the writer George Jean Nathan said.

Are they driven to madness or do they seek it? "As an artist you get a milk glass full of insults, which counters whatever joy you might get," the painter Julian Schnabel said. "But success doesn't need people agreeing with you. The making of the art is the thing that's the joy."

Some artists learn to use their imbalances productively. "What garlic is to salad," the sculptor Augustus Saint-Gaudens said, "insanity is to art."

THREE WOMEN IN A MAN'S WORLD

1) The Soldier

"I've come to lead your army to victory."

"You're not an officer."

"I will be when you give me an army."

"And, I hate to point this out, but you're a child."

"No matter."

"And a girl."

"Look, are we going to argue about this all day long? Or are we going to get it in gear and kick the British out of France?"

With no military training and no army, Joan of Arc became the inspirational leader of France in the early 1400s. She rallied troops who had known nothing but defeat and led them to victory against the British.

No other girl warriors fought in the French army. Or if they did, they hid themselves as men and did not dare to assume leadership.

Wounded in battle, Joan refused to retreat. Mad or a saint, she fought on when others ran. She said she was guided by angels who wanted to make Charles the king of France. What were those angels thinking to sacrifice such a noble woman for such an ignoble cause?

Charles, for whom Joan fought so hard, was a stupid, cowardly leader who did not merit her sacrifice or the throne. He betrayed Joan. He retreated from battle. Joan of Arc rode to the rescue. She built a bridge across a river to take the English, who occupied Paris, from the rear. The king dismantled the bridge and prevented her greatest victory.

The angels should have chosen a better king. Joan, so brilliant in battle, could have chosen a better cause. The French were no more worthy of angelic intervention then the British or the Burgundians, who sometimes fought for the French and sometimes against them.

Joan, called a saint by the common people, was branded a witch by her enemies. She was the first teen rebel and the first French patriot, trying to unify a land weakened by feudal lords. She was also the first protestant, taking her guidance directly from God, not through the church.

Captured, she could have been rescued by arms or ransom, a common practice in those times. The French nobles refused, as did the king and the church. Such is gratitude for a girl whose saintly qualities threatened their grip on power.

The daring often die young to the relief of those trying to maintain the status quo. Joan of Arc was the rebel whose cause betrayed her.

Joan answered the angels' call. Or called herself to a life of grand adventure. Either way, Joan was one of the most amazing women in history. Yet when the *Wall Street Journal* took a survey to gauge how well Americans knew their history, the paper found that 12 percent of the respondents thought Joan of Arc was Noah's wife. Oh, how the mighty have been misplaced.

2) The Politician

Cleopatra, who was Greek not Egyptian, was not born to rule Egypt. Her brothers were. By tradition in the Ptolemy family, she was born to marry her brothers. But her brother-husbands kept dying, a traditional way for younger brothers to move up the royal ladder. Drowning and poison were popular ends to short reigns.

Cleopatra proved more adept than her brothers at staying alive — and a smarter, more resourceful ruler. When she assumed the throne after the deaths of her brothers, Cleopatra turned a country on the verge of financial and political collapse into a strong, prosperous nation, so wealthy that she was able to finance the dreams of glory of her Roman suitors.

Cleopatra sided with Mark Antony in his power struggle against Octavius. Antony was the lesser general. But with Cleopatra's help, he came one battle shy of pulling victory from defeat.

If Antony had ruled Rome and Cleopatra had kept Egypt, what would have happened to Jesus? Without the Roman conquerors to persecute Jesus and his followers, would the entire history of Christianity have been changed? Instead, Cleopatra lost her throne and her life, ending Greek rule of Egypt.

Centuries later, Cleopatra inspired a rare feat from the actress Vivien Leigh (Scarlett O'Hara in *Gone with the Wind*). Leigh played double Cleopatras on Broadway in 1952, alternating shows each night between George Bernard Shaw's *Caesar and Cleopatra* and Shakespeare's *Antony and Cleopatra*.

3) THE PRETENDER

Deborah Sampson fought in the American Revolution disguised as a man, calling herself Robert Shurtleff. When she was wounded in battle, she took a knife and dug the bullet out herself, to prevent other soldiers from discovering her secret.

A second wound led to a fever, and the army doctor revealed Shurtleff as a woman. Oddly enough, when Sampson returned to her Massachusetts home, she stayed in uniform and pretended to be another man, this time calling herself Ephram Sampson.

She made quite a handsome man, and several town women suggested their availability in marriage. At this point, Ephram reappeared, out of uniform, as Deborah and married a man. That settled it, although she occasionally returned in uniform to perform military drills on the lecture circuit.

Old soldiers fade away, or sometimes they just change their clothes.

PART 3

❧ TWENTY-TWO ❧

GET TWISTED:
MOMENTS THAT HAVE MADE
MY LIFE A LITTLE STRANGER
THAN IT HAD TO BE

Section 1
SEVENTEEN STRAY THOUGHTS

1) No man is an island. But several men are peninsulas.
2) The smartest person you know has done something so incredibly stupid even the dumbest person you know wouldn't do it.

3) As we all know, there are a lot of people who don't have a clue. This means there are other people who have more than their share of clues. But if they're so smart, how many clues do they need?

4) If what doesn't kill you makes you stronger, does that mean that what does kill you makes you incredibly stronger—right up until the moment it kills you?

   And if you've been made so strong at that point, how come it can kill you? Maybe if you were a little weaker, you wouldn't have died.

5) You know how people say, "Many thanks"?

   Can't they be more specific?

   "Six thanks to you, pal."

   "I really appreciate what you did. Eight thanks."

   "That was great, a 9.5 thanker."

   Maybe not, thanks anyway.

6) The ultimate math problem, as passed along by the poet Dennis Morton: Exactly how long will I live?

7) Don't try to clear things up. You'll only confuse people.

8) Speak normally and carry a medium-size stick.

9) If you get it wrong the first time, maybe they won't ask you to do it again.

10) If at first you don't succeed, play the outfield.

11) If at first you do succeed, sit down until the shock wears off.

12) Go west, young man. When you hit the ocean, turn right.

13) All that glitters is not gold. But enough of it is to keep collecting the stuff.

14) If you have nothing good to say about anyone, you will get invited to a lot of parties.

15) Do men who wear Speedos and women who buy bikinis not own mirrors?

16) How about a little sympathy for the plight of the suffering succotash? Why must it suffer so? Can't we envision a better world where people sit down to a heaping bowl of happy succotash?

17) If the Arrow Collar Man had married the Old Dutch Cleanser girl, who would their children be? The Campbell Soup Kids is my guess.

Section 2
CITY DESK? GET ME REWRITE!

Working as a newspaper editor is like having a front-row seat at the parade of human oddities. Writing funny books gives you the freedom to rewrite history anyway you want.

When California was going through its energy crisis in 2001, President George W. Bush said the federal government wouldn't help the state out. We all knew why: California had voted for Al Gore in the presidential election.

That seemed unfair. After all, a few million Californians *had* voted for Bush. Why should they be left powerless along with the Democrats?

With a little ingenuity, the feds could have turned the power back on only for the Republicans, while leaving the Democrats in the dark, where Bush thinks they've been all along.

While working for a newspaper, you receive strange press releases. Two of my favorites:

1) The invitation from a TV network to a gala Emmy party, at which reporters could interview a lineup of big stars. At the end of the invite came this mind-bender:

"This press release may contain 'forward-looking statements' within the meaning of the Private Securities Litigation Reform Act of 1955. Any forward-looking statements are subject to certain risks and uncertainties that could cause actual results to differ materially from those stated."

In other words, none of the big stars they promised in the press release would actually show up.

"Forward-looking statements" are the lies lawyers make for you when you don't want to be held accountable for promises you have no intention of keeping even if they were keepable, which they are not.

2) From the National Barley Foods Council came this provocative thought: "When it comes to using barley, many still think soup."

Had to admit, that was me. The council suggested I expand

my barley consciousness with barley muffins, barley-stuffed mushrooms, and barley-lettuce-and-tomato salad.

But when the barley boys told me to take a glass jar, fill it with pearl barley, and bring it along as a hostess gift the next time I was invited anywhere, I had to shout, "Soup's on."

You may be too unimportant to remember this, but when Nancy Reagan was First Lady, her astrologer said, "I don't do ordinary people, just important people."

Because the future is important—at least to some people—now presenting: the Two-Way Astrology Column.

If you are one of the important people, you'll know who you are. All ordinary people, well, *we* know who you are.

JANUARY 9

Important People: A tall dark stranger will carry you away for romance on the Costa del Sol.

Ordinary People: A tall dark stranger will repossess your '93 Pontiac Firebird.

JANUARY 10

Important People: Love will be yours today.

Ordinary People: Don't go into the supply room if that weird guy from accounting's in there.

JANUARY 11

Important People: The planets are lined up in your favor. Good day to invade that pesky little country with the dreadful table manners.

Ordinary People: The planets are lined up. Good day to duck.

If you want to become famous, find two other people to take the trip with you:

Harpo, Chico, and Groucho
Curly, Mo, and Larry
Tinkers to Evers to Chance
Peter, Paul, and Mary
Jesus, Joseph, and Mary
The Father, the Son, and the Holy Ghost
The Three Wise Men
Three Dog Night
3M
Three Blind Mice
Sex, drugs, and rock 'n' roll
Peace, love, and understanding.

Physicists can't travel deep into space to study the nature of the celestial phenomenon known as black holes. But they might gain a better understanding of black holes by studying teenagers.

So much matter can be absorbed into a black hole that the large one at the center of the Milky Way contains three million ex-suns, yet it's not full — exactly like a teenager's closet.

If God played favorites, you'd have to reason that he preferred the insects, having made so many more of them than he did of us and giving them more ways to survive us then we have to survive them.

One of the nastiest and oldest: the scorpion. Fossil scorpions have been found that date back 400 million years, and their disposition hasn't changed much either.

When I lived in Phoenix, every night I'd walk the fence line around our house with my black light and my baseball bat killing scorpions, which glow in black light. The only other time you see a scorpion is after it stings you.

I'd kill twenty a night, and then the next night twenty more. Never did get rid of the scorpions but did improve my bat speed considerably.

Section 3
NEWS FROM THE FUTURE

Considering how weird things already are, can life get any stranger in the future? Here's a look inside the Secret Headlines of the Future file of the *New York Times-Enquirer*, where they follow the time-honored newspaper tradition of predicting the future by making it up.

2008: Life discovered on other planets. Aliens turn out to be no better looking than we are.

2009: Secret discovered to eternal life. Faced with an eternity of *Seinfeld* reruns, mankind gives secret back.

2010: God apologizes for his little mistakes. "Fleas! What was I thinking?"

2011: Wealthologists discover: Best things in life not free! It's the next-to-best things in life that are free. Best things cost more than you can afford and require an appointment.

2012: Peace accord reached. Apples and oranges get together at last; realize how much they have in common.

2013: Computer programmer proves Thomas Edison wrong: genius not 1 percent inspiration, 99 percent perspiration. Genius actually 1.7 percent inspiration, 98.6 percent perspiration, .4 percent bad math.

2014: Government declares future illegal. Having discovered that terrorists and other freedom-haters *plan* their attacks before they can be carried out, co-presidents Jenna and Barbara Bush declare the future off-limits to everyone but official members of the Bush Land Security team.

2015: Last Democrat in America agrees to go quietly. New two-party system emerges: one for Republicans who can afford the dues; other party drinks heavily.

Section 4
OUT OF HOLLYWEIRD:
STRAY THOUGHTS WHILE SITTING IN THE
DARK WAITING FOR MOVIES TO START

When I was a film critic, I'd see a couple hundred movies a year. If I was lucky, they were either great or awful. It's the sincere in-betweeners that bore you witless—unless you train your razor-sharp mind to wander off in the dark.

When Hollywood releases a Director's Cut of a movie, the film always plays longer. If only they released the Critic's Cut instead.

Coming soon to multiplex near you: the Critic's Cut of *The Matrix II*, now with seventy-seven fewer minutes, the way it always should have been.

Shakespeare in Love turned out to be a surprise hit, probably because it was a wonderful, hilarious movie. But the producers took a big risk with a movie title that might have scared off anyone with bad lit-class flashbacks.

If I'd been running the studio, we would have called the movie, *There's Something About Juliet*, or maybe *Free Verse Willie*.

Here's a fun game to play at the movies: Find the wacky moments that make no sense. Filmmakers count on their audience being too dumb to catch the loony tunes. Guaranteed: the worse the movie, the more wacky moments you'll find.

Let's play a round with *Dante's Peak*, the volcano disaster flick starring Pierce Brosnan. A few of my favorite nutty moments:

1) When a small town is threatened by the about-to-explode volcano, all the parents rush into an emergency evacuation meeting—and leave their kids at home.

2) As the volcano blows, a National Guard unit pulls into town to rescue the last five survivors. The soldiers jump out of their trucks and run down the street carrying their rifles. What are they going to do—shoot the volcano?

3) Brosnan, Linda Hamilton, and the kids have to escape over a lake filled with deadly acid in a tiny motorboat. But the acid in the lava-water eats away the blades of the motor. No problem. Brosnan rolls up his jacket and rows them to shore. The metal-eating acid has no effect on the Brosnan jacket.

Got to love the movies: even when they don't entertain you, they entertain you.

Remember when Tom Cruise and Nicole Kidman were married and everyone wondered: Can two of the world's best-looking, most-talented millionaires find happiness together—or even somewhat together?

Turns out they couldn't. Big surprise in Hollywood, where it seems the only people who don't get divorced are the ones who never get married.

But before Tom and Nicole went their separate ways, I imagine they had the typical marital spats all couples face as they try to build a life together.

"Nicole, darling, you can't keep spending money like it grows on trees."

"But, Tom, it does grow on trees."

"Oh, right, guess I forgot. It's just that you're so beautiful, I can't think straight."

"Tom, don't be ridiculous. You're even more beautiful than I am."

"Oh, right."

So what went wrong? The big threat to their marriage played itself out on every celebrity TV show and in every magazine and newspaper: Nicole was, gasp, a good inch taller than Tom.

Can this marriage survive? Well, no it couldn't. Was it heightism that drove them apart? Sure, why not? That's as good as any other Hollywood excuse.

We can help Nicole and other Xena-like women celebs who are thinking of diving into the celebrity wedding game, with our Smaller/Taller Scale:

Marriages on the rocks waiting to happen (smaller than Nicole): Johnny Depp (five-foot-nine), Mel Gibson (five-foot-nine), Mark Ruffalo (five-foot-nine), Philip Seymour Hoffman (five-foot-nine), Jackie Chan (five-foot-eight), Jack Black (five-foot-six), David Spade (five-foot-six), and Danny DeVito (five-foot).

OK to marry these guys, Nicole (they're big enough, unless their publicists are stretching the truth): Brad Pitt (five-foot-ten), Matt Damon (five-foot-ten), Adam Sandler (five-foot-ten), Ewan McGregor (five-foot-ten), Viggo Mortensen (five-foot-eleven), Woody Harrelson (five-foot-eleven), Jude Law (five-foot-eleven), John Travolta (six-foot), Heath Ledger (six-foot-one), Kevin Costner (six-foot-one), Will Smith (six-foot-one), Adrien Brody (six-foot-one), Keanu Reeves (six-foot-one), Ben Affleck (six-foot-two), John Malkovich (six-foot-two), and Tim Robbins (six-foot-five).

Here's the theater marquee for Old Movie Night down at the Twisted Multiplex:

Red Planet Mars. Mars Needs Women. Women in Love. Love with a Perfect Stranger. Stranger Than Paradise. Paradise for Three. Three Men and a Little Lady. The Lady in Red.

And here's how they run the space-saving ad in the paper: Red Planet Mars Needs Women in Love with a Perfect Stranger Than Paradise for Three Men and a Little Lady in Red.

Section 5
LOVE THOSE WACKY ADS

They're all quite mad in the ad agencies, and rich — a combination that can produce real-life ads that score high on the Wacky-O-Meter:

Here's a creative crew going nuts trying to sell Levi's Dockers:

"If you took some Levi's jeans, added a BMW convertible and a well-worn Cartier Tank watch and a Bass Weejun loafer, plus the way it feels to really trounce your tennis instructor" (wait, there's more) "and then whipped it all together in a Cuisinart, what you'd get is Levi's Dockers."

Forget the pants. Where can I get that blender?

Safeway supermarkets went the sincerely insane route in this TV commercial for their fish markets:

The spot opens on a burly fisherman unloading crates of fish from his boat. "It used to be fish," he tells us. "Now it's seafood. But it's still fish to me."

The fisherman goes on to tell us that, whatever you call it, the fish tastes better since his wife started buying it fresh at Safeway.

Here, at last, is the miracle supermarket that can provide the guy who caught the fish with fish that's fresher than the fish he caught. Also, they can sell fish to the guy they bought the fish from for less money than they paid him for the fish they bought.

That's a trick. Why is it when you try to make sense out of TV commercials, you end up sounding like Dr. Seuss?

In a magazine ad for Silk Reflections stockings, a beautiful woman looks dreamily off into space while showing off her legs in the park.

Her boyfriend's there too, a guy who wears a tuxedo when he goes to the park, looking dreamily at his girlfriend and rhapsodizing:

"Reflections on Lindsay. She hates small talk . . . never lost an umbrella in her life. And what legs . . . Lindsay's legs."

What I want to know is: How does he know she never lost an umbrella in her life? Even when she was little? When she used to date other guys?

Let's face it—there's only one person who would know for sure about her amazing umbrella-maintenance program, and that's Lindsay herself.

But she won't tell us because "she hates small talk." So Lindsay, babe, if you're as smart as he thinks you are, lose the dope.

Section 6
THE WORLD'S FUNNIEST PEOPLE:
LIBRARIANS

I spend a lot of time doing research in libraries, where I've discovered that librarians have a secret world, telling jokes to each other that they don't share with outsiders.

That's why they all whisper—so you don't find out how funny they are. Here are seven of my favorite Secret Librarian Jokes:

1) A woman decided to have her portrait painted. She told the artist, "Paint me wearing a diamond necklace, diamond earrings, an emerald bracelet, and a Rolex watch."

"You're not wearing any of those things," the painter pointed out.

"It's in case I die before my husband does," the woman explained. "I'm sure he'll remarry, and I want his new wife to go crazy looking for the jewelry."

2) A little boy prayed to God, asking for $100. When he didn't get the money, he wrote God a letter asking why.

When the post office saw the letter to God, they sent it on to the White House. An aide showed the letter to the president, who was impressed and sent the boy $5, thinking that was enough money for a child that young.

When the little boy got the $5, he sent God a thank-you note:

Dear God: Thank you for sending me the money. I noticed that you sent it through Washington. As usual, those thieving idiots deducted $95.

3) Alcohol and calculus don't mix. So don't drink and derive.

4) Don't you know the king's English? Their language can drive you nuts, which seems to amuse the librarians who compiled these English oddities:

If vegetarians eat vegetables, what does a humanitarian eat?

If teachers taught, why don't preachers praught?

Fill in that form by filling it out.

The barn burned down when it burned up.

Isn't it odd that a slim chance and a fat chance are the same thing?

People recite at a play and play at a recital. They have noses that run and feet that smell. But there is no egg in eggplant and no ham in a hamburger. Double that for a pineapple, which contains neither pines nor apples.

If you're only a little sorry, how come you can't make an amend?

If you have some odds and ends and throw away all but one of them, what do you have left, an odd or an end?

5) Your computer has just received the Amish Virus. Since we have no electricity or computers, you are on the honor system. Please delete all your files. Bless thee.

6) If librarians were put in charge of corporate mergers:

Federal Express and UPS would merge, and the new company would be called: Fed-Up.

PolyGram Records, Warner Brothers, and Keebler would form: Poly-Warner-Cracker.

3M and Goodyear: Mmm-Good.

Knott's Berry Farm and the National Organization of Women could join forces to become: Knott NOW.

7) If you think American kids don't have a clue, check out these questions and answers from a school exam for British teenagers:

Q: Name the four seasons.

A: Salt, pepper, mustard, and vinegar.

Q: What's a major disease associated with cigarettes?

A: Premature death.

Q: How do you keep milk from turning sour?

A: Leave it in the cow.